living
untethered

Beyond the Human Predicament

MICHAEL A. SINGER

New Harbinger Publications, Inc. | Sounds True

Publisher's Note

This publication is designed to provide accurate and authoritative information in regard to the subject matter covered. It is sold with the understanding that the publisher is not engaged in rendering psychological, financial, legal, or other professional services. If expert assistance or counseling is needed, the services of a competent professional should be sought.

Character names originating in the Star Wars series, some of which are registered trademarks of Lucasfilm Entertainment Company Ltd. LLC, are used in this book pursuant to the Fair Use Doctrine for purposes of commentary and other transformative uses. No sponsorship or endorsement of this book by, and no affiliation with, the trademark owner are claimed or implied by the author or publisher.

Whispers from Eternity by Paramahansa Yogananda is published by Self-Realization Fellowship, Los Angeles CA.

All Bible verses are from the King James Version unless otherwise specified.

A copublication of New Harbinger Publications and Sounds True

Copyright © 2022 by Michael A. Singer
New Harbinger Publications, Inc.
5674 Shattuck Avenue
Oakland, CA 94609
www.newharbinger.com

Cover and interior design by Amy Shoup; Horse illustration by Sara Christian; Acquired by Catharine Meyers; Edited by Jennifer Holder

Library of Congress Cataloging-in-Publication Data on file

Printed in the United States

24   23   22

10   9   8   7   6   5   4   3   2

To the Masters

Contents

PART I

Conscious Awareness

CHAPTER 1

Awareness of Self

Sitting on a planet spinning through vast outer space for a handful of years—in the broadest sense, this is the human predicament. Earth has been here for 4.5 billion years, yet each of us is limited to roughly an eighty-year ride on the planet, give or take a few years. We were born onto the planet, and we will leave it when we die. That is simply the truth. What is not such a hard and fast truth, however, is what our few years on Earth are like. Undoubtedly, life on the planet can be a very exciting experience. It can bring enthusiasm, passion, and inspiration at every turn. When it unfolds that way, every day can be a beautiful adventure. Unfortunately, life on Earth rarely unfolds exactly as we want it to, and if we resist, our experience can be quite unpleasant. Resistance creates tension and anxiety, and it makes life a burden.

To avoid this burden and be able to fully embrace life, wise ones throughout the ages have taught the importance of accepting reality. Only by accepting reality can we work with the flow of life as it passes by and create a better world. All of science is based on studying reality, learning her laws, and then working with those laws to improve our lives. Scientists can't deny reality; they must fully accept reality as the starting point of their endeavors. To fly, we must fully embrace the law of gravity, not deny its existence. The same is true in the spiritual realm. Teachings such as surrender, acceptance, and nonresistance form the basis of a deeply spiritual life. But these concepts can be difficult to grasp. In *Living Untethered,* we are embarking on a journey into the sheer reasonableness of acceptance and the great gifts it promises: freedom, peace, and inner enlightenment. Acceptance is best understood as nonresistance to reality. Try as you may, no one can make an event that has already happened not have happened. Your only choice is to accept the event or resist it. During our journey together, we will explore how and why you make this decision. But first you have to understand who is within that has the power to decide.

You are certainly *in there*; you have an intuitive sense of existence inside. What is that? It is awareness of Self, the most important topic we could ever discuss. Since we're going to take a deep dive into the spirituality of acceptance, we must start by understanding who is in there accepting or resisting.

There are many ways to approach the nature of Self. Let's go slowly and start with something very simple. Imagine someone comes up to you and asks, "Hi. Are you in there?" How would you respond? No one would actually say, "No, I'm not in here." That would be the ultimate non sequitur. If you're not in there, who responded? You're definitely in there, but what does that mean?

To isolate what "you in there" means, imagine you're shown three different photographs. The photos are held up one after the other, and then you're asked, "Though the photos changed, was it the same you who saw all three of them?" Your response would be, "Of course it was the same me." Very good; that helps us get our bearings. From this simple exercise, it's clear that you in there are not what you look at; you are the one who's looking. The pictures changed; you who saw them stayed the same.

It's not hard to understand with photographs that you are not what you look at, but there are some objects we identify with more than others. For example, our bodies. We identify with our bodies enough to say, "I'm a forty-three-year-old woman who is five foot six." Is that really who you are in there: a forty-three-year-old, five-foot-six-inch female body? Or is the body something you in there are aware of? To sort this out, let's start with your hand. If you were asked whether you can see your hand, you would say, "Yes, I see my hand." Okay, but what if it got cut off? Don't worry about the pain; just for a moment imagine it's gone. Would you still be there? Wouldn't you notice that your hand is gone? It's like the changing photographs: When the hand was there, you saw it. When it was gone, you saw it was gone. You in there who "sees" did not change; what you were looking at changed. Your body is just another thing you see. The question remains: Who is in there doing the seeing?

Note that we didn't have to stop with the hand. Surgery has become so advanced that, with the help of a heart-lung machine and other medical devices, surgeons could remove a great deal of your body—and the same sense of Self would still be in there, aware of the changes. How could you be your body if it changed that much, and you in there stayed the same?

Fortunately, to help you realize you are not your body, we don't really need to go that far. There is a much simpler, intuitive way to approach this. Surely you've noticed that your body didn't look the same when you were three, ten, twenty, or fifty years old. It certainly won't look the same when you're eighty or ninety. But isn't it the same you in there looking at it? When you were ten years old and you looked in the mirror, did you see what you see now? No, but wasn't it you looking—then and now? You've been in there the whole time, haven't you? That's the core, the essence, of everything we're discussing. Who are you? Who is in there looking out through those eyes and seeing what you're seeing? Just like when you were shown the three photographs, you were not any of the photos—you were the one looking at them. Likewise, when you look out at the mirror, you are not what you see—you are the one who sees it.

Little by little, through the use of these examples, we are revealing the nature of Self. Your relationship to what you see is always one of subject-object. You are the subject, and what you are looking at is the object. There are many different objects coming in through your senses, but there's only one subject experiencing them—*You*.

CHAPTER 2

The Conscious Receiver

Once you recognize that you're in there, you're going to notice that objects around you tend to distract your consciousness. A neighborhood dog barks, someone walks in the room, you smell the aroma of coffee, and your awareness is drawn to these objects. On a daily basis, you are so distracted by external objects that you rarely remain centered on *You,* the conscious receiver of these objects. Let's take a moment to examine the real relationship between this conscious receiver and the objects it is distracted by.

To look at this scientifically, you are not even looking at the outer objects. Right now, you are not actually looking out at what you see. What's happening is that rays of light are bouncing off the molecules that make up the outer objects. These reflected rays are hitting your eyes' photoreceptors and being transmitted back as messages through your nervous system. These messages are then rendered in your mind as an image of the external objects. You are actually seeing the objects inside, not outside.

We are slowly peeling back the onion to see what it's like to be you. Things are certainly not what they appear to be. Even science backs that up. It's like you are sitting inside looking at a mental flat-screen monitor that is imaging the world in front of you. You are obviously not the object you are looking at; after all, you are not even looking at the actual object. If you work your way back, the question becomes: "Who am I in here looking at a mental image of what is in front of me?"

There was a great saint from India, an enlightened master named Ramana Maharshi. His entire spiritual path was to every moment persistently ask: "Who sees when I see? Who hears when I hear? Who feels when I feel?" *Self-realization,* the term for enlightenment the yoga master Paramahansa Yogananda used, means you have fully realized who you are in there. The entire spiritual journey back to the seat of Self is not about finding yourself—it's about realizing you are the Self. Even in a Judeo-Christian sense, if somebody asks whether they have a soul, the correct answer is, "No, you don't *have* a soul—you in there, the consciousness, *are* the soul." Thus, "Who are you?" becomes the quintessential question. You can't free yourself until you understand who it is that's bound. Likewise, you can't understand acceptance until you understand who is resisting.

Let's continue our exploration of Self. Earlier we discussed that when you were young, you looked out through your eyes and saw a certain reflection in the mirror. Later in your life you saw a very different reflection. From that point of view, how old are you? Not how old is your body. How old are you in there who's looking out through those eyes at your body? If you were in there when you were ten, if you were in there when you were twenty, if you're going to be in there on your deathbed noticing that you're dying, then what age are you in there? Don't answer that question, just let it touch you at a very deep level. Are you willing to let go of traditional concepts about your age?

Let's do another interesting experiment. Imagine you're looking in the mirror right after taking a shower. Do you see the reflection of a male or female body? What if suddenly, via some mysterious power, it changes? Somehow the body parts change. If you were a male, you're now looking at a female. If you were a female, you're now looking at a male. Would it still be the same you in there looking at that body? Would it still be the same consciousness that has always looked out through those eyes now seeing a very different body? You would probably be saying, "What happened? What's going on here?" Nevertheless, it would be the same you having the entire experience. So what gender are you in there? You in there, who has no body parts, can't have a gender. All you can have is awareness that when you look out through your eyes, the body you're looking at has a certain form and shape. That form and shape might be male or female, but you who notices are neither.

The question remains, who are *You,* the awareness that intuitively knows you're in there? Your body has an age and your body has a gender, but those concepts are irrelevant to the one who notices the body. If you look at a tall, one-hundred-year-old vase, does that make you tall and a hundred years old? The same is true of race. Your skin may be a certain color, but the consciousness that notices this has no color at all. You are not your body; you are the one who notices the characteristics of your body. You are the conscious awareness within that is looking at all of this. The question is: *Are you willing to let go of who you thought you were?* Because who you thought you were is not who you are. The same inner being is looking at your body, your house, your car. You are the subject; all the rest are objects of consciousness.

Let's turn to something a little lighter. At night you go to sleep, and you often dream. You wake up in the morning, and you say, "I had a dream." That statement is actually very deep. How do you know you had a dream? Do you merely remember the dream or were you actually in there experiencing it? The answer is very simple: you were in there experiencing it. The same you who looks through your eyes and sees the outer world was experiencing the events occurring in the dream. There's only one conscious being in there, and you are either experiencing the waking world or the dream world. Note that when describing your interactions with both worlds, you intuitively use the word "I," as in "I was flying through the clouds with my arms open wide, then I suddenly woke up and realized I was in my bed."

In *The Yoga Sutras of Patanjali,* which is a very ancient yogic text, Patanjali discusses the topic of deep, dreamless sleep. He says that when you go to sleep and there are no dreams, it's not that you are not conscious, it's that you are conscious of nothing. If you spend time contemplating this, you're going to find that you're always conscious in there. Even people who get knocked unconscious, or go into a coma, often come back and tell us what they were experiencing. People have near-death experiences in which they leave their bodies and come back to tell about it. Whatever the source of these experiences, the same you in there experienced them and were able to describe what you experienced. How can you call that not being conscious? Medically, what we call "conscious" has to do with awareness of our external surroundings. However, the concept of whether you in there are consciously aware of anything—that's another story altogether. You're always conscious. You've been conscious from the beginning. You're aware of whatever you focus on, internally or externally. Who are you? Who is that consciously aware entity inside?

CHAPTER 3

Living Inside

We are back to the most basic truths of your life: you're in there, you know that you're in there, and you've been in there all along. This raises some interesting questions, such as, when the body dies, will you still be aware of being? Isn't that an interesting question? Don't get excited, we're not going to answer that for you. Eventually, however, there will be someone who provides that answer: *You*. You are guaranteed to personally find out someday whether you will be there after the body dies. Why do people have so much trouble with death? It's got to be one of the most exciting aspects of your life. It's truly a once-in-a-lifetime experience! That is what's waiting for you at the time of death. After that final moment, either you are going to be there or you are not. If you're not there, don't worry. It's not like, "Oh my god, I'm not here. I don't like this." No. You're not there, so it's not going to be a problem. The other alternative, however, is much more interesting—what if you are there? Then you're going to find out what it's like to explore a whole other universe where you don't even have a body. Let's not talk about it further because it runs into people's beliefs, concepts, or views about the subject. Let's just let it be something to look forward to as the ultimate once-in-a-lifetime experience.

The reason some people have so much trouble with death is because they identify with their bodies. As if that's not enough, they also identify with their cars and houses. People project their sense of self onto things that are not their self. When they do that, they feel afraid to lose those things. As you work your way through your inner growth, you won't identify with these outer objects anymore. You'll identify with the deeper sense of self within.

Now that it's clear that you're in there, it becomes reasonable to ask: What do you do in there? Even more relevant, what's it like in there? What an interesting question to ask: What's it like in there? If people answered honestly, most would say that it's not always so much fun in there. In fact, sometimes it's downright tough. What's that all about? This is where we get down to a real honest discussion about inner growth. Most people don't realize that it can always be nice in there. Take the nicest it's ever been: holding your first child, the day of your wedding, your first kiss, winning the lottery. Recall that state, then increase it multifold and have it be that way all the time—except that it keeps getting higher. That is what you are capable of experiencing inside. That's the truth. It is really beautiful in there, but something is messing it up. Imagine walking into a house that has dirt, banana peels, and pizza crusts all over the place. It happens to be a beautiful house, but no one took care of it. It can be beautiful again, but some work needs to be done. This is exactly the situation inside you. In fact, that is why we're on this inner exploration. Everybody wants the same thing: they would like it to be nice in there.

People do all kinds of things trying to make it nice in there. Some run around trying to have exciting experiences, find fulfilling relationships, or even take the edge off with drinking or drugs—all for the same reason. The problem is they're approaching the issue in the wrong way. They're asking *how* to make it nice in there, while the more relevant question is *why* is it not nice? If you find out why it's not nice, and you get rid of that, you're going to find out it can be really nice in there. Life doesn't have to be a game of, "Since it's not nice in here, I need to find things that will compensate for that in order to feel a little bit better." That is what everybody's doing. They are trying to find people, places, and things in the outside world that will unfold in a way that makes it more comfortable inside. People are trying to use the outside to fix the inside—better to find out why it's not nice inside to begin with.

CHAPTER 4

The Three-Ring Circus

"I'm in here. I'm conscious, and what I am conscious of is that it's
  not always so nice in here."

That honest statement is a wonderful launching pad for continuing our exploration of Self and the power of acceptance. What is it you experience that sometimes makes it nice inside, and sometimes makes it very difficult? There are only three things you experience in there, so let's take a look at them. First, you experience the outside world coming in through your senses. There's a whole world out there, and what's in front of you comes in through your eyes, ears, nose, and senses of taste and touch. When it comes in, it's either a pleasant experience, an unpleasant experience, or a just-passing-through experience. Thus, the outside world is one of the things you deal with that has a profound effect on your inner state.

As overwhelming as the outside world can be, it's not all you experience inside. You also have thoughts in there. You hear the thoughts saying, "I don't know if I like this. I don't even understand why she did it." Or perhaps, "Wow! I'd like to have a car like that. I would go for long weekend rides in the country." If you're asked who is saying all this inside your head, you'll probably say it's you. But it is not you. Those are thoughts, and you are the one who is noticing the thoughts. Thoughts are just another thing you notice in there. You notice the world coming in from outside, and you notice the thoughts that are generated inside.

Where do thoughts come from? We're going to discuss that at length later, but for right now, understand that thoughts and the outside world are two of the three things you experience inside. The third thing you experience is your feelings or emotions. There are feelings that come up suddenly, like fear. Your mind can say, "I feel scared," but if you didn't actually *feel* scared, the impact would be much less. It's the fact that you actually experience the emotion of fear that causes the problem. Some feelings are pleasant: "I felt love. I felt more love than I have ever felt before." You like that feeling. Other feelings are unpleasant: "I'm feeling fear, embarrassment, and guilt coming up all at the same time." You don't like that, do you?

We've already come a long way in our exploration of Self. We've proven you're in there, and the strongest proof is you know that you're in there. This is your *seat of awareness*. Anytime you get lost, just stand in front of the mirror and say, "Hi, are you in there?" Wave at yourself, and realize, "Yep, I see somebody waving. Who am I that sees that?" This is a way to center back to your seat of awareness. While you stand there, notice what else you're aware of. Notice your surroundings coming in through your senses, your thoughts passing through your mind, and any emotions that arise in your heart creating feelings of comfort or discomfort within. These three inner experiences are the arena in which your consciousness plays the game of life on planet Earth.

Bottom line, you don't stand a chance in there. The constant barrage of these three experiences is like a three-ring circus going on inside all the time. The effect is so overwhelming it's like a conspiracy against you. The outside world has a major influence on your thoughts, and your thoughts and emotions will generally line up. It's very rare that your mind will be saying, "I don't like this," and your heart will be feeling tremendous love. Let's say Fred passes by and your mind says, "I don't want to see Fred. I'm not comfortable seeing him after the argument we had last time." You will start to feel fear. You were doing fine until an event came in from the outside, took over your thoughts, and generated difficult emotions. You get sucked into that overwhelming experience. Now if you're asked, "What's it like living in there?" you would probably say, "It's pretty intense. I get lost a lot and struggle to be okay." It's not all that much fun, is it?

Buddha said all of life is suffering. He wasn't being negative. All of life *is* suffering. If you're rich, poor, sick, healthy, young, or old—it doesn't matter. There certainly are times when you're not suffering, but the vast majority of what's going on is you're just trying to be okay. That's what it boils down to. You will at some point realize that's all you've done your entire life—try to be okay. That's why you cried when you were little; you weren't okay in there. That's why you wanted a certain toy; you thought it would make you okay. That's why you wanted to marry this special person. That's why you wanted to go to Europe or Hawaii for a vacation. You get to the point where you realize all you're ever doing in there is trying to be okay. First you think about what will make you okay, then you go out and try to make it happen.

What does it even mean to try to be okay? For one thing, it means trying to make your thoughts and emotions easier to live with. There are nice ones, and there are not-so-nice ones. You like the nice ones. That's what you're struggling with. You want your thoughts to be positive, uplifting, and beautiful. The problem is there's an outside world of reality that can come in and cause your thoughts and emotions to be very difficult. This is why life can be overwhelming.

This interaction with the world, your thoughts, and your emotions raises some very interesting questions. What are these three things, and where do they come from? How much control do you have over them? Why do they sometimes make you feel good and other times make you feel bad? We're going to explore these questions in great detail. When we're through, you'll realize that what really matters is not the thoughts, the emotions, nor the outside world. What really matters is *You* in there, who is experiencing these things. How are *you* doing? What we'll see is that you in there are higher than any experience you've ever had. The one who is seeing all this is the most beautiful thing in the whole universe. If you ever find your way back to the seat of Self, that's what you're going to discover. This is what Christ taught you, what Buddha taught you, what all the great spiritual masters of every tradition have taught: The Kingdom is within you. You in there are a very great being made in the image of God, but to know that, you have to free yourself from all the inner commotion.

CHAPTER 5

Exploring the Nature of Things

Your entire life is composed of consciously experiencing the three objects of consciousness (the outer world, the thoughts, and the emotions). Now we are ready to explore the origin and nature of these experiences. By understanding where they come from, they will lose some of the distractive power they have over you. You will then better understand your tendency to accept or reject them. We study these objects of consciousness not solely for the knowledge we gain, but also for the freedom we attain.

Let's discuss the nature of the world passing before you. Every moment that passes before you comes and goes like the frames of a motion picture. The moments never stop; they just keep flowing through time and space. Where did all these moments come from? Why do you experience them the way that you do? What is your true relationship to what passes before you?

Perhaps even more interesting than the outer world, we're going to explore the nature of the mind and the emotions, including how and why they keep changing the way they do. Though all three of these objects of consciousness are constantly changing, you are the persistent being that is always there experiencing them. What is your nature? What is it like to sit back and be conscious of being conscious? That is what all spirituality is about. When you are no longer distracted by any of the three great distractors, your consciousness will no longer be pulled into those objects. The focus of consciousness will very naturally remain in the source of consciousness. It's like a flashlight shining on various objects. Instead of looking at the objects being illumined, if you look at the light itself, you will realize it is the same light shining on all the different objects. Likewise, it is the same consciousness that is aware of all the objects passing before it, both outside and in. You are that consciousness. When you pull back to that source of awareness, it is the most beautiful thing you will ever experience.

That is the journey before us—to free ourselves from the distractions that keep drawing us away from our greatness and leave us struggling with life. As you come to understand the nature of these objects you are struggling with, you will very naturally be able to release the hold they have on you. This act of letting go is what is meant by "acceptance" and "surrender." There is a state of great peace within you that cannot be disturbed by the world, your thoughts, or even your emotions. These objects can continue to freely exist, but they will no longer dominate your life. You will be free to fully interact in life, but you will do so out of a sense of love and service, rather than fear or desire.

Now you understand the underlying purpose of this book: for you to learn how to let go of the three great distractors and return to the source of your being. As you will see, this is the only way you can fully enjoy your time here on Earth. This is what it means to be *Living Untethered*. It doesn't take forceful practices to return to your core. The highest path is learning through your daily life to gradually let go of what is distracting your consciousness. By accepting instead of resisting, you will eventually attain a permanent seat of clarity—it's called becoming established in the seat of Self. You will be living in the most beautiful energy you've ever experienced, and it will never stop. During every moment of your life, there will be a beautiful flow of energy that keeps rising within you.

We are going to approach this process of freeing yourself in a very scientific, analytical manner. By doing so, you will become so comfortable with the three objects of consciousness passing before you that you will no longer have to devote your life to controlling the experience. You will see that these passing objects represent the lower aspect of your being: body, mind, and emotions. In drastic contrast, you can learn to establish yourself in the higher aspect of your being: the seat of conscious awareness. You can live your life in a state of complete freedom and happiness.

Are you ready? Let's embark on our journey into the exploration of our outer world, inner world of mind and emotions, and the consciousness that experiences it all. Let's learn more about this path of acceptance of what passes before us.

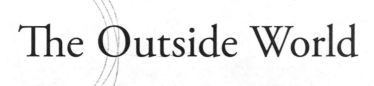

PART II

The Outside World

CHAPTER 6

The Moment in Front of You

Keeping perspective is essential at every stage on our path toward inner freedom. The solid ground we keep coming back to is that you are in there; you know you're in there; and you've always known you are in there. But you don't focus on the fact that you are in there because you are too absorbed in what is going on both inside and outside you. You get lost in the objects of consciousness, instead of focusing on the source of consciousness. Spiritual awakening is about untangling consciousness from the objects of consciousness. To do this, it will help tremendously to understand the nature of the objects of consciousness you deal with each day.

We begin our exploration with the outside world. What you receive in through your five senses is a significant part of your daily experience. You are inundated each day with an unending stream of sights, sounds, tastes, smells, and touches. If we are going to explore what it is like to be *You,* the conscious being living within, we need to take the time to thoroughly understand the outside world since it makes up such a major part of your life. What is actually out there, where did it come from, and what is your relationship to it?

Let's begin by exploring your relationship to the world around you. We'll start by making a statement that you probably will not agree with: *The moment in front of you right now has absolutely nothing to do with you.* Before you disagree, just look at the moment in front of you. Don't do anything with it. Don't meditate on it or try to be positive about it. Just notice that there is a moment in front of you. Now, look to the left; there's a different moment in front of you. Look to the right; there's yet another moment in front of you. Those moments were there before you looked at them, and they will still be there when you're done looking. How many moments exist in the world right now that you are not looking at? How about in the entire universe? You must admit that those moments have nothing to do with you. They belong to themselves and their relationship to all that surrounds them. You didn't create them, and you don't make them come and go. They are just there. The moment in front of you is just another moment in the universe that exists even when you are not looking at it. It is completely impersonal.

Nonetheless, the moment in front of you doesn't seem impersonal; it seems very personal. That is why it can cause so much trouble. You suffer when the moment in front of you is not the way you want, and you rejoice when it matches your preferences. As we will explore in later chapters, this is because of something you are bringing into the moment—it is not something intrinsic to the moment itself. All moments in the universe are simply moments in the universe; you are the one bringing your personal preferences into these impersonal moments and making them seem personal.

This is our first encounter with seeing how difficult it is to surrender our habitual way of looking at things. We are perfectly willing to admit that what is going on in Timbuktu right now has nothing to do with us. Likewise, we have no problem admitting that the rings of Saturn, the big storm on Jupiter, and the sands of Mars have nothing to do with us. In other words, more than 99.99999 percent of the universe has nothing to do with us, but somehow the .00001 percent does. Which .00001 percent does? The part that's in front of you. Somehow, because you're looking at it, it's no longer part of the impersonal universe. It has become personal.

The problem is, you have made a really big deal out the moment in front of you throughout your life by bringing your personal preferences into that moment. Notice that the billions of people who are not looking at the moment in front of you don't have any problem with it. They couldn't care less about it. It's not stirring up their thoughts, and it's not stirring up their emotions. When you're no longer experiencing that moment, it generally won't be bothering you either. Instead, the moment you turn to next will be bothering you. "Why is she sitting there?" "Who's she talking to?" "The lights are way too bright." All of a sudden this new moment starts affecting you because you're looking at it. The truth of the matter is, it existed exactly the same before you looked at it. *One of the most amazing things you will ever realize is that the moment in front of you is not bothering you—you are bothering yourself about the moment in front of you.* It's not personal—you are making it personal. There are countless moments unfolding in the universe at any given time, and your relationship to all of them is exactly the same: you are the subject, they are the object.

Once you realize this truth intellectually, it still won't look that way in your everyday life. To help, let's take a field trip out to Fisherman's Wharf in San Francisco, overlooking the beautiful Pacific Ocean. While you're gazing out there, ask yourself whether what you see in front of you has anything to do with you. You see waves, you see spray, you may even see some whales or sea lions. That just happens to be what is unfolding in front of you at that moment. If you had come on a different day, or even a different hour, what you'd see would be quite different. But this would not bother you. It would only bother you if you came to the wharf with some personal preferences: "I want to see a whale." "I want to see the giant waves people told me about." With these preferences, you will have a very different experience than someone who simply came to see what the Pacific Ocean looked like that day. One person can simply enjoy the experience; the other has to struggle to make the experience match their personal preferences.

In the case of the ocean, it is not difficult to see that the moment before you has nothing to do with you, and you have the right to simply enjoy the experience. Because you don't generally identify yourself with the ocean, this is easier to do than with the rest of your life. But let there be no doubt, your relationship to what is in front of you is always the same, whether you are looking at the ocean or at your life. These moments are just what happens to be happening at that particular time and place in the universe where you happen to be standing. None of it is personal.

But since you seem to take the moment in front of you so personally, let's continue our exploration of the outside world by looking at where that moment came from and why it is the way it is.

CHAPTER 7

The World You Live In

If you want to know where the moment in front of you came from, it makes sense to go to our scientists. They have inquired about this as far back as Aristotle and Plato. From the beginning of our existence, humans have pondered: *Where did all of this come from? What made it? Why is it here?* If we ask scientists today, they will say that what you are looking at when you look at the outside world is actually a blending of much smaller objects. Your eyesight and all your senses are averaging molecular structures. As we've already explored, you are not actually looking out at the world; it is coming into you through your senses.

To see how this works, let's examine the nature of color. When you look at the world, it certainly appears to have color. But other than light, itself, objects have no color. The only reason you experience color is because the light bouncing off the objects has color. You see this when examining a prism. If you shine light through a prism, you will get different colors. It is called the *electromagnetic spectrum.* Light has different wavelengths, and you perceive each visible wavelength as color. Remember ROY-G-BIV: red, orange, yellow, green, blue, indigo, violet. They make up the colors of the visible part of the light spectrum. When light waves hit a physical object, the different atoms and molecules of that object absorb some frequencies of the light and reflect others. Objects themselves have no color; it is the light reflecting off them that has the different colors we perceive. This is a perfect example of how truth is not always what it appears to be. We will see this time and again as we examine the true nature of what consciousness experiences.

Scientists used to think the atom was the smallest possible unit, and it could not be subdivided any further. Today we understand that an atom is composed of electrons, neutrons, and protons. It forms the basic unit of everything we look at every day. We could stop right here and have some fun with the very personal way we look at things. For example, what exactly do you mean when you say you like something? What is it you claim to be liking? If you like the color of the wall, that's like saying you like part of the electromagnetic spectrum and not other parts. Likewise with any outside object. Do you really like some atoms and not others? It gets a little weird, doesn't it? This truth is very powerful because all you're ever looking at is a bunch of atoms with light bouncing off them.

After hundreds of years of study, scientists have told us that atoms get pulled together into molecules through the laws of covalent and ionic bonds. This may sound complicated, but they are really just the laws of magnetism determining which atoms will bond together. These laws, in turn, determine what you will see in the outside world. Certainly at this level you can see that it's not personal. It has nothing to do with you. You don't decide which atoms or molecules bond together naturally. It's been going on all over the universe for billions of years.

Our scientists have told us there are currently only 118 different types of atoms in the known universe, with 92 of them occurring naturally on Earth. These are what make up the periodic table of elements. The periodic table represents the building blocks of what you are seeing and interacting with every moment of your life. This is not just on Earth. All the stars, the planets, and everything everywhere that we've encountered are made from these basic elements. Many of you have studied the natural sciences in school, but what if you apply what you've learned to your everyday life? What's in front of you is simply the accumulation of mass amounts of atoms being pulled together by the laws of nature—it's all just science, nothing is personal. Becoming personally offended by the flow of atoms as they pass by you is so illogical. Why would you get upset because of how a bunch of atoms joined together? Don't worry, before we're done we will have fully explored the phenomena of getting personally upset over a bunch of atoms.

From here, it gets really interesting because the question becomes, "Where did the atoms come from?" Now we're inquiring about the origin of matter. Understanding where the atoms come from can give you a sense of your place in the universe. All that's happening in your daily life is your consciousness is looking at electrons, neutrons, and protons that have pulled together to form atoms and molecules. Since this is the world you live in, let's take time to explore where it all came from. Understanding this has the potential to alter your entire view of life.

CHAPTER 8

The Origin of Matter

If you study the origin of matter, you'll find that scientists throughout the world pretty much agree on a basic model of creation. They have an understanding that about 13.8 billion years ago there was a giant explosion called the *big bang*. Prior to this explosion, it is thought that all the galaxies and everything within them, all the mass and matter of the universe, fit into a space smaller than an atom. This is modern science speaking, not some crazy theory. With awe and appreciation as our goal, let's explore how the science of creation can serve to liberate us spiritually.

After the big bang, the energy expanding out was so hot that it didn't have any shape or form. It was just unbridled radiation. Within a fraction of a second, subatomic particles began to form from this energy field. No elements as we know them could form because the radiation was too hot, and it was expanding out at the speed of light. Thus the entire universe was without form for about 380 thousand years. After that, the radiation cooled down enough to where the fundamental forces of gravity and electromagnetism could pull the subatomic particles together to form the first atoms. We know these subatomic particles as electrons, neutrons, and protons. It was all born from the primordial energy field and the subatomic particles emanating from that field. Modern science calls this the *quantum field*, and quantum physics is the science that studies these subatomic particles and how they create matter as we know it.

The first atoms were hydrogen because it is the simplest structure: one negative electron and one positive proton. Because of the force of magnetism, these particles attracted each other to form an atom. As hydrogen atoms began to form, masses and masses of thick hydrogen gas clouds accumulated. As these clouds thinned out, subatomic light particles called photons started to escape, and that was the beginning of light as we know it. Interesting that the Bible says, "In the beginning... the earth was without form, and void; and darkness was upon the face of the deep" (Gen. 1:2). That is pretty close to how science sees it. In those beginning times, no light could escape from the ultrathick gas clouds. Once the expansion thinned the clouds out enough, suddenly "Let there be light: and there was light" (Gen. 1:3). It's amazing, the similarity of the beginning of creation as told in Genesis and as presented in modern, scientifically based cosmology.

Now that we see where hydrogen atoms come from, we can explore the source of the other elements that make up our world. As the expansion slowed down even more, another one of the fundamental forces came into play—the force of gravity. Gravity, of course, is the force that has the effect of pulling together objects that have mass. Since hydrogen atoms have mass, as the atoms were pulled closer together, the gravity became so strong that it fused two atoms into one. When two hydrogen nuclei fuse into one, a helium atom is created. This process of fusing lighter elements into heavier ones is called *nuclear fusion*, and it's been going on throughout the universe for hundreds of millions of years.

It is worth noting that every single time this fusion of two atoms takes place, there is a tremendous release of atomic energy. All of a sudden, nuclear explosions began taking place throughout the universe, releasing powerful radiant energy. This is the birth of what we call the primary stars. A star is born by the fusing together of hydrogen atoms, which releases tremendous amounts of energy and leaves helium atoms as its byproduct. You can think of helium as the ash left behind by this hydrogen fusion process. Wherever the clouds of hydrogen gas were thickest after the big bang, the first primary stars started to burn. That is literally where stars come from. Every star you look at to this day was born through the hydrogen fusion process.

Though this all started 13.8 billion years ago, we have scientific evidence of it today. Stars are being born right now, and we can observe the process. If you have binoculars strong enough to see the Orion Nebula, you will see gases with stars shining inside. Nebulae, like the Orion and Horsehead, are not just beautiful pictures of glowing, colorful gas clouds. They are nurseries for stars. Stars are being born inside those gas clouds via the exact same process that happened 13.8 billion years ago when the first stars were created. Stars are born and, as we shall see, also die in a cosmic cycle of life mirroring what is going on here on Earth.

In our exploration thus far, we have a universe limited to hydrogen and helium gases and brilliant burning stars that light up the cosmos. But the outer world we interact with each day is much more complex. Where did the rest come from? To understand this, we must first take a closer look at the life cycle of a star. As the hydrogen gases within a star keep fusing, gravity pulls the produced helium into the core of the star because helium is heavier than hydrogen. This increases the gravitational pull of the core enough to offset the outward radiance of the explosions caused by hydrogen fusion. This is how the star stays stable. What happens when the star runs out of hydrogen to fuse? The star will start to die.

In the early stages of the dying process, any hydrogen remaining outside the core will ignite and expand outward to create a "red giant" star that is many times the size of the original star. To put this in perspective, when a star the size of our Sun begins to run out of hydrogen to burn, it will expand into a red giant large enough to swallow the Earth. But don't worry, scientists estimate that our Sun has enough hydrogen to burn for another five billion years.

Meanwhile, as a star stops fusing hydrogen, the gravitational pull of the helium core will become greater and greater because there are no longer fusion explosions to offset it. The star will start to collapse into its core. Depending upon the original size of the star, its core will either drift off into space, or the increased force of the gravity on the core will become great enough to begin fusing helium into more complex elements, such as carbon. The fusion process of these more complex elements will reignite the star, even hotter than before. Depending upon the size of the star, these "death throes" can go on again and again. Cycle after cycle, more and more complex elements will become the byproduct of fusion of lighter elements, and eventually the star will begin to collapse again as it runs out of fuel. Every time this death cycle takes place, more and more elements of the periodic table are created.

How many of these cycles of death and rebirth a star will go through is dependent upon the original size of the star. The larger the star, the greater the gravitational force exerted during its collapse, and thus the greater the force available to reignite the fusion process of the more complex elements. In most stars, this process will stop when the byproduct of fusion is iron (element 26 in the periodic table). This is because iron absorbs more heat during fusion than the fusion process creates. Thus, iron will not sustain a fusion reaction. Large stars will progress until they have cores of iron surrounded by shells of the remaining elements from the previous cycles that were not fully burned. This is how the lighter elements on the periodic table (1 to 26) were created, all the elements from hydrogen to iron.

As interesting and educational as all of this is, remember that the purpose of this discussion is to see where "the outside world" comes from. As amazing as it seems, the elements that make up our world were forged in the stars. Take your body, for example. We have already explained where all the elements that make up your body come from—they are the direct byproducts of what makes the stars shine. Almost 99 percent of the mass of the human body is made up of six elements: oxygen, carbon, hydrogen, nitrogen, calcium, and phosphorus. All of these elements are lighter than iron, and thus were produced by the burning of commonplace stars. We know all of this as fact, not theory. Scientists have studied stars at all stages of the stellar life cycle, and we know what they are made of. Regardless, some people ask, "Don't these scientific facts challenge my belief that God is the creator of the universe?" An appropriate response would be, "Of course not. They merely show you *how* God created all the structures in the universe."

The stars are the furnaces that were used to create the universe. Every single atom you interact with was created in the stars, and at this very moment billions and billions of stars are forging more elements. In Pittsburgh we have steel furnaces that are so hot we can forge steel. We use that material to build our giant skyscrapers. Likewise, the stars are the furnaces that have forged the atoms we interact with every day. Hopefully, you will never again look up at the stars in the same way.

CHAPTER 9

The Power of Creation

Now that we've seen how ordinary stars create the lighter elements of our world, we can move on to an even more fascinating topic: how the heavier elements on the periodic table are created, like gold, platinum, and silver. The heavier elements are all those with an atomic number greater than iron (26). Iron forms the dividing line because it absorbs more heat than it releases during fusion. As such, iron doesn't emanate enough heat energy to stop a star from collapsing. Unless the original star was exceptionally large to begin with (a "red supergiant"), it will finally die when it gets to an iron core.

What happens during the death of a red supergiant star is one of the most amazing events in the known universe, and it provides the energy source needed to create the heavier elements. If the star is large enough before its collapse, the intensity of the collapse can actually crush the atoms in the core. Instead of fusing the iron atoms together, this tremendous force pushes their electrons into the nucleus itself. Since electrons are negatively charged and the protons in the nucleus are positively charged, they attract each other and form neutrons, which have no charge. Once this happens, all that is left of the iron core is a mass of tightly packed neutrons. There are no atoms left—no electrons and no protons. The intensity of the collapse of this large star down to just neutrons has destroyed the structure of matter as we know it.

What is left is a neutron star, and it is tiny in size but enormous in mass. Neutron stars are physically about the size of a city but have a mass that is more than three-hundred-thousand times heavier than the planet

Earth. The density of a neutron star is so great that if you brought a teaspoon of it down to Earth, it would weigh twelve trillion pounds.

The amount of energy released by the collapsing of the star's core down to just neutrons is so powerful that it creates a colossal explosion called a *supernova*. This explosion is so enormous that a single supernova emits more light than the combined light of all the billions of stars in its galaxy put together. It is the brightest, most powerful explosion we have discovered in our universe.

As it turns out, the enormous energy force generated during a supernova explosion is precisely what is needed to create the rest of the elements we interact with each day. What the force of gravity was unable to do during the creation of the lighter elements, the massive explosion of a supernova is able to do—fuse the heavier elements. The next time you look at your gold wedding ring, or open a tin can, reflect on the fact that these elements required the combined power of billions of stars to come into existence.

You are surrounded by the myriad objects you interact with each day. There are giant skyscrapers and tiny paper clips that effortlessly come in through your senses. At their root, every single one of these objects is made of atoms. You have just taken the time to understand where all these atoms come from and how you did not create them—they were created in the stars. This should serve to humble you and leave you in awe of the power of creation manifesting before you. Hopefully, this deep sense of humility and awe will assist you on your spiritual journey toward freedom and liberation.

It's Not Personal

We just explored where the world around you comes from. It began with the big bang, and then all the different types of elements were created through the process of atomic fusion. When stars explode at death, all the matter that built up in their outer shells gets blown out into interstellar space. Carbon, oxygen, silicon, gold, and silver were all floating around as clouds of elements in space, then gravity pulled them together to form the planets. This is how the planet Earth formed with its ninety-two natural elements, all of which were forged in the stars. This process has gone on for over thirteen billion years, and everything you interact with each day is composed of this "star dust," including your body. This is the truth, and we should remember and contemplate it regularly.

Let's come back to where we started this discussion. We began with the fact that there is always a moment in front of you. Just open your eyes, and there it is. Where did it come from? Now we know. The moment in front of you came from the stars. The atoms were baked together in the solar furnaces, then pulled together into this mass we call Earth. You studied what happened next in science class. The elements joined together to form stable molecules, such as H_2O, based on the laws of electromagnetism. Because of the interaction of these laws, there's water in the oceans. As other more complex molecules formed, they created the primordial soup from which living organisms formed. Every part of every cell in your body is composed of elements created in the stars, billions of years ago.

This explains where your body came from, but it does not explain where *You* came from. You are not made of atoms; you are the consciousness that is aware of the objects that are made of atoms. Your body may be the result of the long process of Darwinian evolution, but what about you in there? Where did you come from, how did you get in there, and why is it the way it is in there? The natural sciences may explain the outside, but what about the inside? This is exactly what we will be exploring in the coming chapters.

What science has discovered about reality should give you more respect for creation, not less. The fact that we are able to explain these phenomenal events that took place should leave you with a sense of awe. Just look at how it ended up after 13.8 billion years. Dare to look at what's in front of you in this light. Now that you know where it all came from, pay attention. What's in front of you is a very holy thing, all of it.

Now consider whether this process of creation had anything to do with you. Were you around causing any of this to happen? Will you be around for the next billion years causing all that is going to happen to take place—everywhere? Of course not. The universe is a phenomenal system of cause and effect. What was, causes what is; what is, causes what will be. This has been happening from the beginning of time throughout the universe. Every single moment in front of you took billions of years with everything happening exactly like it did to manifest as it is.

To fully understand what this means, it helps to look at a simple example from your family history. If your great-great-great-grandmother didn't meet your great-great-great-grandfather, you're not here. That's simply the truth. Let's take a moment to tell a story of how they met so you can see how dependent everything is on everything else. The story begins all the way back with the dinosaurs. After a fierce storm in what is now South Central Florida, there was a big dinosaur lumbering around. When this dinosaur put its big footprint down into the wet soil, it caused a gigantic imprint in the mud. Over time, rainwater accumulated in this deep imprint, and the earth began to erode around it. Eventually, the water area grew so large it became what we now call Lake Okeechobee.

Millions of years later, the Mayaimi tribe settled by that lake because of the fresh water, fish, and other animals. Centuries passed, and Spanish settlers built a small town on the edge of the lake. Your great-great-great-grandmother was a descendent of the Mayaimi, and your great-great-great-grandfather was visiting the small Spanish settlement. One day while it was pouring rain around the lake, your great-great-great-grandfather was drinking in the local saloon. He was so drunk when he stepped out of the saloon, he never noticed your great-great-great-grandmother walking by sopping wet. Just as he stumbled down the stairs falling drunk to the ground, your great-great-great-grandmother slipped in the mud and fell right on top of him. Well, they looked at each other, started laughing, and it was love at first sight. The rest is history.

In other words, if the dinosaur hadn't walked there millions of years ago, and if the Mayaimi tribe hadn't settled there, and if the Spaniards hadn't built a town there, and if it hadn't been raining that day, and if grandpa hadn't fallen down drunk at the exact spot where grandma slipped in the mud—you're not here, and neither are a lot of other things. Every single thing is the result of every single thing that ever happened throughout time and space. You're not the doer; you are the experiencer of reality.

If this is true, and it is, then it's pretty silly to think, "It took 13.8 billion years for this moment to get here, and every single thing had to happen exactly as it did—but I don't like it." That's funny. It's like saying that you don't like that Saturn has rings.

Now do you see why we took the time to explore where what's in front of you came from? It has nothing to do with you; it is the result of trillions of factors that caused it to be the way it is. This is our first encounter of what surrender and acceptance really mean. You don't surrender the outside world—you totally accept it. What you surrender is your personal, made-up judgment of it. If you were asked whether it's okay with you that Saturn has rings, you would probably look very puzzled and say, "What's it got to do with me? That's a crazy question." The truth is every single thing is that way. It has nothing to do with you. It has to do with the forces that caused it to be the way it is, and those forces stretch back billions of years. The total acceptance of this truth is surrender. You must let go of the part of you that thinks it has the right to like and dislike the result of billions of years of interactions. Surrender is letting go of the part of you that is not living the truth. That is true surrender.

Eventually, you will come to realize that the moment in front of you is a very holy thing. Our scientific exploration of where that moment came from is actually very spiritual. Quantum physicists are exploring how the entire universe is emanating from an omnipresent, undifferentiated field of energy—the quantum field. They are showing us how everything is made of light. That used to be a strictly spiritual concept. Our scientists are our priests. They are teaching us how the underlying force of creation created creation. Science shows us that every moment before us is worthy of great respect. A spiritual person understands these truths, ingrains them into their being, and lives their life accordingly.

If it took 13.8 billion years for the moment in front of you to get there, and it took 13.8 billion years for you to end up in front of that moment, every moment is indeed a match made in heaven. Nobody else is standing there experiencing exactly what you're experiencing. Truth is, no one ever did, and no one ever will. That exact moment will never be here again. All moments just keep passing through time and space. You are being given a unique show that took billions of years to create—it's right in front of you, and you're complaining about it. We all think we have very good reasons to complain. The intention of this journey we are on together is to take away those reasons, whatever they are.

The moment in front of you is a gift from creation. There are shapes, colors, and sounds. There are people and lots of things to do. It's not that way on Mars, nor on any place we have seen thus far in studies of the universe. But we don't live our lives with a constant sense of awe and appreciation. That's why these discussions about cosmology and quantum physics are spiritual. They are taking away your right to make everything personal when it's not personal. Your consciousness may be aware of the moment in front of you, but you did not create that moment. You are simply being given this wonderful opportunity to experience a moment in creation. It took billions of years to get here—be sure you don't miss it.

People make such a big deal out of science versus God, as if the two are at odds with each other. The real problem is that people don't truly believe in either. If you believed that science explains the creation of all things, you would live your life with the constant awareness that everything you are interacting with is emanating from the quantum field, pulling itself together into atoms and molecules, then appearing as the form before you. You would not like it or dislike it; you would be in awe of it. Likewise, if you really believed God was the creator of all things, you would live in awe and appreciation of the marvel of the Divine Creation. You would not like it or dislike it; you would be blown away that it even exists.

You live in a world where a seed falls on the ground, and it has a built-in chemist that knows how to break down the molecules of dirt and water, mix them with sunlight, and combine those substances into a corn-stalk or a tree. You're taught that this "intelligent chemist" is the complex DNA molecule. Where did this amazing molecular structure come from? All its elements were forged in the stars and then naturally got pulled together into the DNA structure by the four fundamental forces (gravity, electromagnetism, and the strong and weak nuclear forces). Human intelligence had nothing to do with the creation of DNA, yet DNA is responsible for all the plant and animal life on Earth. We live in a world that is so perfect it should constantly blow our minds. But we are so lost in making it all personal that we miss both the greatness of science and the greatness of God.

We began this exploration by asking what it's like for you in there. You know you're in there—what is the nature of the experiences you're having? To answer this, we explored the origin and nature of the outside world in which you live. Hopefully, you have more respect and appreciation for it right now. That moment in front of you is special. You might want to practice appreciating it and notice the effect that has on your life.

Next we're going to work with the mind and its thoughts, then the heart and its emotions. They don't come in through your senses, but they are certainly things you experience. As we comb through each layer, it's going to become easier and easier to let go—to accept and surrender. Remember, you are not surrendering life; you are surrendering your resistance to life. We can use the term *mindfulness* to mean that you are always conscious of what is really going on around you and inside you. You're not just conscious of the appearance of things but also their true nature: where they come from, why they are the way they are, and what it took for them to manifest before you. Mindfulness is a natural, effortless process once you let go of personal distractions. Instead of thinking that the moment in front of you has to be a certain way, you start thinking that it's pretty awesome the way it is. In fact, it's amazing that it even exists.

From now on, everywhere you look and everything you interact with, be sure to say, "Thank you." And be sure to pay tribute to the stars. They are not just romantic things twinkling in the night sky. They are the furnaces of the universe. They have created everything for you. Can you thank them? Can you appreciate this truth, and understand that you didn't do anything to deserve the trees, the oceans, and the sky? You don't even know where *You* came from. You're just in there experiencing this amazing gift unfolding before you. *This is spirituality—coming into harmony with reality, instead of your personal self.*

PART III

The Mind

CHAPTER 11

Empty Mind

As a conscious being, you are aware of the world coming in through your senses. But your awareness is not limited to that outside world. You also have inner experiences. Sometimes when the world comes in, it makes you feel good. Other times, it makes you feel bad. Since the outside world is really just structures of atoms, why does it have that inner effect on you? How could a bunch of atoms get you all jumbled up inside? What's going on?

You are capable of experiencing three distinct things: the outside world, the mind, and the emotions. Now that we have deeply examined the nature of the outside world, let's start our journey into understanding the second object of consciousness: the mind. What is mind? We all know what mind is. We're in here, and we experience it every day of our lives. In the simplest sense, mind is a place in which thoughts exist. We have thoughts all the time: "Why is he driving so slow? I'm going to be late. Now what am I going to do?" Undoubtedly these are thoughts, but where do they exist? They certainly don't exist in the outside world. Scientists are not able to read your thoughts, as hard as they have tried. But you can. There's not a machine they've ever made, even for billions of dollars, that can read your thoughts. Yet you can, effortlessly. That's a pretty amazing power you have.

Take a moment to digest that fact. Your consciousness has the ability to be aware of things that machines can't detect: thoughts and emotions. These objects of consciousness surely exist, but not in what we define as the "physical" world. Our scientists have shown us that the whole universe comes down to energy. Thoughts and emotions are simply energy vibrating at such high rates that machines can't detect them. Someday they might be able to. Machines couldn't detect gamma rays, X-rays, or even infrared light until we made machines that could pick up those subtler vibrations. Scientist didn't then classify these higher-vibration objects as something alien to our world. They simply expanded the definition of the electromagnetic spectrum to include them. It's not that the higher vibrations hadn't always been there, we simply hadn't been able to detect them.

Likewise, your thoughts are there and have always been there. What if a scientist told you, "No, your thoughts are not there. I can't detect them, so they don't exist." You'd walk away and laugh. You know your thoughts are there. You, the same conscious awareness we've been discussing, have the ability to pay attention to, or not pay attention to, the thoughts being created at this higher vibration of energy. Through the years, people have called this higher range of vibrations the *mental plane*.

Many questions come up regarding the topic of mind. For example, what are thoughts and where do they come from? Since scientists don't have direct access to your thoughts, only you can answer these questions. You're in there, and you have the ability to look at your mind. You even use the terms "my mind" and "my thoughts." You say, "I had a terrible thought the other day. My thoughts are really bothering me lately." How do you know you had a terrible thought? How do you know that your thoughts are bothering you? You are in there, so you know what it's like to be in there experiencing thoughts. You can think of mind as a very high-vibration field of energy in which thoughts can be created. Mind is not the thoughts. Mind is the field of energy in which thoughts are capable of existing. Just as clouds are not the sky, but they exist in the sky and are formed out of the substance of the sky, so thoughts are not the mind, but they exist in the mind and are formed out of the substance of mind.

Buddhists talk about *empty mind*. In the purest sense, that is what we are referring to when we use the term "mind." It is a field of energy with nothing in it. There are no thoughts. There's just an absolutely still, formless field of energy we call "mind." This not conceptual; you can go there. Meditators who have gone deep understand this. You just rest in void, in empty mind. You're there, but there are no thoughts. It's just completely quiet, completely empty. It's like a powerful computer that has no software on it. The computer has great potential, but it doesn't do anything. That is what empty mind is. It's not stupid; in fact, its latent capabilities are enormous. It is simply still, not creating thoughts. Basically, that is what Buddhists mean by empty mind, and it is our starting point for understanding mind.

The outside world exists independent of this field of mind. Whether the mind is still or the mind is noisy, the planet continues to spin on its axis and all the galaxies continue to float through space. The energy that makes up the physical plane is at a grosser vibration rate than the energy that makes up the mental plane. From your own personal experience, you know that consciousness is capable of being aware of both the physical plane and the mental plane at the same time.

Now that we've examined the concept of empty mind, let's begin the process of forming objects in the field of mind. In order for you in there, consciousness, to be aware of the physical plane, you were given a physical body to house the five senses that pick up sight, sound, smell, taste, and touch. This body is a gift that the stars gave you and that evolution perfected. Because of the senses, the vibrations from the outside world come in. They pass through the sensory receptors, up the sensory nerves, into the brain, and then manifest in the mind where you experience them. This rendering of the outside world is one of the most basic functions of mind. It's very much like watching a ball game being played in California while you're in Florida. The actual physical light and sound vibrations are picked up by the cameras at the game. They are then digitized and transmitted to a receiver at your home. The received signals are then rendered onto your flat-screen TV. It seems like you are looking at the game, but you are not. You are looking at the rendering of the transmitted signals that the cameras picked up.

It's amazing how much this parallels what is happening when you "see" the world around you. Your senses pick up the different vibrations from the outside world, just like a camera's sensors do. In the case of your senses, however, you can pick up five different vibration rates, not just sight and sound. Your senses convert the different vibrations into electrical nerve impulses and transmit them to the brain. The signals are then rendered in the mind's energy field to as closely as possible replicate the original physical source. You become aware of what is going on in front of you by being aware of its mental image rendered in your mind. Just like you become aware of the ball game in California by being aware of what is rendered on your TV screen in Florida.

You're not out there in the world. You're inside. You're way back inside. Though the world is happening everywhere, you only experience the part that is picked up by your senses and rendered in your mind. Mind is no longer empty—it has formed its energy into the exact image of what is within the scope of your senses. As we discussed, you are not looking out into the world. The outside is being reproduced in your mind, and you are looking at that mental image. It's really not that different from when you are dreaming. In the dream state, images are being created in the mind, and you are looking at them. The waking state is the same, except that the mental images are being generated by the senses instead of by the mind itself. These mental images that form in the mind are like the images that form on your flat-screen TV. The screen was blank, but now it has taken the form of the ball game in California. Your mind was empty, but now it has taken the form of the outside world around you.

Your mind is so brilliant. Your flat-screen TV has a digital signal processor that takes the received digital signal, decodes it, and renders it onto the screen and through the speakers. Your mind takes the encoded nerve impulses and reproduces the entire scene in front of you, including depth perception, as well as adding touch, smell, and taste. It renders all this detail made out of the higher energy vibration of the mind. This exact rendering of the outside world is one of the primary functions of your mind. It allows you in there to experience the outside world. The mind is such an amazing gift. It is naturally formless, yet it can create forms that are more brilliant than those made by the most powerful computer. Mind is really the first personal computer. In fact, it is so personal that it doesn't need any external form. Its display screen is inside, its computing and graphics capability are inside, and you don't need a keyboard, mouse, or voice recognition to communicate with it. It is so close to you that it responds to your will and the slightest impulse from your heart.

We have now gone from empty mind to a mind that renders the outside world so you can experience your surroundings. Experience is the nectar of life. You're in there, and you're capable of experiencing because of the rendering capability of your mind. Of what meaning is life if you don't experience it? We spent a lot of time discussing how the outside world was created—billions of years of stellar activity resulting in what appears around you. You saw how it was created; now you see how consciousness, which does not belong to the world of form, can experience it—through the miracle of mind.

In truth, consciousness is the most profound miracle. An essence that knows that it knows that it knows. Everything else is something you're conscious of—the true magic is consciousness itself. When consciousness is simply experiencing reality as imaged in the mind, that is what we call *being in the present moment.* At this point in our discussion, there is nowhere else to be. The real world is outside, it is being reflected in your mind, and you are aware of the image right in front of you. In this very simple state, you are experiencing what you were meant to experience: the gift of the moment that's being given to you. It comes in, and you learn from it simply because you experienced it. There are no distractions; there is just total oneness with the moment in front of you.

Everyone has had some rare moments like this. Perhaps it took a beautiful sunset to bring you to such a state of one-pointed consciousness. You were driving around a corner and, all of a sudden, the sun was setting with beautiful purple, orange, and magenta. It was the most beautiful thing you had ever seen, and it completely blew your mind. What does that mean, "It blew your mind"? It means there was nothing left in your mind but that image of the sunset. Not the mortgage, not the problem with the boyfriend, not the worries from the past. The only experience you were having was this beautiful sunset coming in through your eyes, rendering in your mind, and merging with your entire being. Your entire consciousness was centered and focused on the experience you were having, instead of being scattered all over the place. It was truly a spiritual experience.

That is what *The Yoga Sutras of Patanjali* describes as the experiencer and the experience becoming one. You have allowed a merger between subject and object. There's nothing distracting your consciousness from what is happening right in front of you. This is the yogic state of *dharana*—one-pointed concentration.

You've had other experiences that approach this state of one-pointed absorption. Sometimes in intimate moments with someone you love, when everything is just right, you lose yourself in the moment. All of a sudden, total beauty and peace come over you. When consciousness merges with the object of consciousness, you can feel the presence of God. In yogic philosophy, the Self is called *sat-chit-ananda,* eternal-conscious-bliss. When Self focuses one-pointedly on a single object, one experiences the nature of Self—total peace, contentment, and overwhelming bliss. This is available to us at any time if we can just learn to enter the undistracted state of one-pointed consciousness.

CHAPTER 12

Birth of the Personal Mind

Why don't we live in an ecstatic state of one-pointed consciousness all the time? What went wrong? What caused the fall from this proverbial garden?

It's very simple: The world comes in and it's beautiful. The very act of experiencing it is tremendously moving when it comes all the way back into you. However, that does not mean it all feels the same. Heat feels different from cold—because it is different. That doesn't mean one is better than the other. They just feel different. Somebody gently touches you, and that feels very different than if they bump into you. Different things are experienced in different ways. The Buddhists say everything has its nature. A coiled rattlesnake comes into the mind as a very different experience than a butterfly landing on your arm. That rattlesnake is giving off its nature—emanating its particular vibration. That vibration is awesome in its own way, but it certainly doesn't create the same inner experience as the butterfly. There's nothing wrong with this. It's very real. What's wrong with having a variety of experiences? If a butterfly landed on you every moment, it would become so normal that it would be nothing. God knew how to create a world that would always be exciting.

Your consciousness actually expands because of the knowledge that flows into it. You are learning and growing through the experiences you are having. This learning through life is true spiritual growth. It is the evolution of the soul. Just like everything you learn makes you smarter, every experience you have makes you wiser. When the presence of a rattlesnake comes into your mind, true, it's not a comfortable inner experience. It doesn't feel the same as a butterfly, but it is just as rich. It is just as important. If you're willing to be open at this level, you're still in the idyllic garden. There are no problems; there are just learning experiences. No matter what happens, you are becoming greater.

Unfortunately, that is not how we live. Something went very wrong. Let's take this fall from the garden in slow motion. First, something comes in; let's start with the rattlesnake. It's not a particularly comfortable experience. In fact, a hissing rattlesnake is meant to be an uncomfortable experience—it may even generate discomfort at a survival level. That would be a strong inner reaction to the outer experience.

But this uncomfortable inner reaction isn't bad, per se—it's just a different vibration. Just like some colors are soothing and others are harsh. Colors aren't bad or good; they are just different vibration rates of the electromagnetic spectrum. You can learn how to be comfortable with these different vibrations. A rattlesnake is not going to stay there rattling your whole life. It's going to come, and it's going to go—and its uncomfortable vibrations are going to go with it. Then something else will happen. You live in a happening place filled with growthful experiences. You are simply in there experiencing creation as it comes in and passes through you.

You don't practice that level of acceptance, however. You in there who is experiencing what's rendering in your mind—you have the ability to resist what is not comfortable to you. You were given free will. You can use that will like inner hands to push away thoughts and emotions if they don't feel right. Surely you have done that. That resistance is an act of will. Will is an innate power you have—it is actually a power that emanates from consciousness. Just as the Sun stays where it is in space, but it emanates rays that have great power, so consciousness remains at its source, but its awareness emanates out onto whatever it focuses on. There is great power when consciousness focuses on something, just as there is great power when the Sun's rays are focused through a magnifying glass. You can feel the power of one-pointed concentration. It is, indeed, concentrated consciousness. That is the source of the power of will.

The power of will plays a very important role in understanding how the mind developed from a place of clarity to one of confusion. You have surely noticed that your awareness does not fall evenly on all objects that render in your mind. You pay attention to some objects more than others. If the vibration of the object was more comfortable or uncomfortable, you either "liked" it or "didn't like" it. This is the foundation of how the personal mind got built: like and dislike. It happens at a very primal level. Basically, it depends on whether you in there have the ability to experience something that comes in without doing anything about it—other than fully experiencing it. This is the ability to allow objects to simply pass through.

If an inner experience is not neutral to you, it draws your consciousness to focus on it. The moment that happens, the things passing through your mind are no longer even; one has stood out from the rest. All it took was for you to focus your consciousness on it. Your consciousness is a force, and you are focusing that force on a particular mental object. When the force of consciousness is focused on a mental object, that object cannot pass through the mind like the other objects. Just as the solar winds interfere with objects passing through space, so focused consciousness is a force that affects objects passing through the mind.

When you focus consciousness on a particular mental form, you impede that form's ability to pass through the mind. The very act of concentrating on it makes it stay in your mind. You know this. When you want to do math in your mind, you concentrate on the numbers so they stay long enough for you to manipulate them. In fact, anytime you want to hold something in your mind, you must focus your consciousness on it so it does not just fade away. Concentration of consciousness freezes forms in the mind so that they don't just pass through. Thus, when you saw a rattlesnake, it might as well have been a standalone item in your mind. The truth is there were trees, grass, sky, and other items rendered in your mind aside from the snake. But you focused your consciousness on the rattlesnake and let the rest pass through. Interestingly, because you focused so much consciousness on it, you froze the experience of the snake in your mind. There was no way you were going to let this uncomfortable experience *all* the way in, and that is the birth of resistance.

Do you know what that means, "letting it all the way in"? We discussed this earlier regarding the beautiful sunset and the perfect romantic experience. You wanted to fully experience these beautiful moments, so you opened up and let them pass all the way into your being. These are the special moments in life, when something touches you to the core of your being. No way this rattlesnake is going all the way in there. You don't have to think about it. Resistance is simply a natural response to something that's not comfortable. You try to keep it at a distance.

Have you ever kept something at a distance in there? Perhaps something someone said that hurt you in the past, maybe an awkward stage you went through when you were young, or even a terrible divorce. Of course you have, but that doesn't mean the event didn't happen. It wouldn't be in there if it hadn't already happened. You can't stop the event from having happened, but you don't have to let it all the way in. Mind is a big place. There's plenty of room between where the experience is first imaged in your mind and where you actually fully experience it. You can use will to keep the mental image at a distance from you. This is a very primal act of resistance.

Now that you have resisted experiencing the rattlesnake, and let the rest of the moment pass through, here comes a butterfly. It lands on you, which is such a beautiful experience that you naturally focus on it. When it starts to fly off, you don't want it to go away, so you use your will to hold on to the mental image. This is what Buddhists call *clinging*. You can't hold on to the butterfly itself because it flew away. So you try to hold on to the mental thought pattern of the butterfly. You push away what it was like to experience the rattlesnake and you cling to what it was like to experience the butterfly. Neither of these mental patterns can finish their natural journey through the mind. Not only do you lose out on fully experiencing them to the depth of your being, you are also left with these mental patterns stuck in your mind. Neither rattlesnake nor butterfly remain before you, but they are left as patterns in the mind's energy field. Such is the power of like and dislike.

Both clinging and resisting keep the mental renderings in your mind. This is very important to understand. Experiential mind was meant to be like a clear TV screen: it renders the image being sent to it. But now you've held on to images that are no longer being generated by the outside world. They got stuck in your mind as mental patterns, and as a result, you're out of harmony with reality. You were in there experiencing the gift of reality; now you are also experiencing the patterns you held on to in your mind. These patterns in your mind are totally different from the patterns in other people's minds. Each person's trapped mental patterns are unique and very personal. They come from how we interacted with our past experiences. Since we've all had different past experiences, and interacted with them differently, the impressions held in our minds are totally different. *This is the birth of the personal mind.*

The problem is: reality is not personal. As you've already seen, we didn't create this world. We are simply experiencing the miracle of creation unfolding around us. Yes, there are rattlesnakes and butterflies in the world, along with lots of other things. But now there are RATTLESNAKES and BUTTERFLIES in your mind, even when they are not actually in front of you. Now that you've held these leftover mental impressions in your mind, reality has to compete with them for your attention. Your ability to fully focus on the outer world is going to be hindered by the constant distraction of these inner impressions.

CHAPTER 13

Fall from the Garden

Resistance is the beginning of what can be considered the fall from the garden. You were just fine being aware of this awesome, everchanging creation. It presented constant gifts of experiences for you to learn and grow from. Take the gift of music. When you are deeply absorbed in music, there are no stray thoughts, only the music effortlessly coming in and feeding the depth of your being. You can be raised to the state of ecstasy while listening to music. When the mind is clear, everything comes in that way. You are either in a heavenly state experiencing what is pouring into you, or you are deeply absorbed in the inner stillness of your being. You have returned to the garden—everything is effortlessly beautiful.

Once you hold on to rattlesnakes and butterflies in your mind, you are unable to stay in that pure state of consciousness. These two mental patterns have become powerfully charged objects that draw your attention toward them. When the mind was clear, what attracted your consciousness was the rendering of the outside world as it passed through. This rendering was very entertaining and fulfilling, but since you had nothing going with it, it just came and went. In contrast, the powerfully charged objects you have held in your mind do not come and go. The world in front of you comes and goes, but these mental objects remain because you are holding them in your mind. Furthermore, since they are differentiated as more important than the rest, your consciousness becomes more distracted by these mental objects.

Everything is no longer equal, and this creates a major problem. Next thing you know, you're walking down the road, and there's a rope.

But the rope no longer feels the same as it would have before you saw the rattlesnake. The rope reminds you of the rattlesnake. What does "reminds you of" mean? It's not a rattlesnake; it's a rope. Nonetheless, when the rope comes in, consciousness now has a choice: pay full attention to the rope that came in, or be distracted by the negative rattlesnake image stuck in your mind. The mind will immediately join these two mental objects together as one, and you will get scared. Scared by a rope? Yes, terrified by a rope.

A similar thing happens with the image of the butterfly stuck in your mind. After the butterfly flies away, you're still focusing on the image in your mind. You're still feeling good about it and trying to hold on to it, even though it is no longer part of your here-and-now reality. Then something new comes in from the outside, like a person walking by. Your mind may be rendering this new image perfectly, but your consciousness is not fully seeing it. Your consciousness is still distracted by the butterfly image that got left in your mind. It used to be that the moment in front of you was the experience you were having inside. Now you have a preference—you would rather experience the mental image of the butterfly than the reality in front of you. There has become a whole new world for consciousness to focus on—the world you built in your mind. That world does not match the reality of creation. That inner world is your own personal creation made out of the mental objects you didn't let pass through. That's what those images in your mind represent: things that happened in the past that you willfully kept in your mind. As we shall see, these impressions are the initial seeds that eventually grew into the self-concept or personal self.

To see this more clearly, let's once again look at the example of a flat-screen TV. When the first plasma screens came out, they had "afterimages." Manufacturers warned that if you paused an image for too long, it would actually burn a shadow of the image into the plasma screen. When the show continued, the old image would still be there. Would you enjoy watching TV like that? You've finished the news, but when you turn on a movie the afterimage of the newscaster is still superimposed on top of your movie. That's exactly what is happening with the butterfly and the rattlesnake. You can no longer clearly see what is going on in front of you because you have these other images on the screen of your mind. You've messed up your screen. You didn't mean to. It seemed innocent to push experiences aside when you didn't find them pleasant. Where do you think they went when you resisted them? They got stored as lasting impressions in your mind.

It is worth looking at the effect of these leftover images in slow motion. In the beginning, the miracle of creation took place. It created form that is coming in through your senses so you can experience it. Apparently, at some point you didn't like certain vibrations, so you pushed them away when they rendered inside. That willful resistance caused them to stay in the mind. This is where *personal* comes from. We said earlier that nothing is really personal. But you have chosen to fill the sanctity of your mind with frozen images from your past. These impressions will stay in your mind and will pull your consciousness toward them. You now have a limited and biased view of reality that will distort all of your experiences for the rest of your life. That is the power of the personal mind.

So far we have only focused on the rattlesnake you resisted and the butterfly you clung to. Those alone are sufficient to distort your experience of reality. But be honest with yourself: How many of these charged impressions do you have? You've done this your entire life. Plus, these stored impressions build on each other. Now that you have a stored rattlesnake impression in there, you can easily get scared by the sound of a baby's rattle. In fact, if the discomfort is bad enough, you may choose not to be around babies. That's a personal preference, and this is where all personal preferences come from. Once you create preferences, they will dominate your entire experience of life.

These impressions that stay stuck in the mind are called *samskaras* in yogic science. They are discussed in the ancient Upanishads texts. How could people know about this thousands of years before Sigmund Freud discussed his theories on suppression? It is because they were meditators. They didn't need someone to teach them about this—they saw it going on in their own minds. If you are quietly centered in conscious awareness, you can see what is passing before you. You are the ultimate experiencer of your mind; you're just not paying attention.

Instead of paying attention, you're getting so uptight about wanting butterflies, and not wanting rattlesnakes, that you're losing your centered awareness. When the world around you comes in and hits, or activates, your stored patterns, you can no longer observe reality objectively. Your consciousness gets drawn into the activated samskaras, and everything becomes distorted. This is the foundation of the *psyche*, your personal self.

What is the psyche? It's something you build inside of the mind that's about you: "I'm the one who doesn't like rattlesnakes. I'm the one who likes butterflies." You just built a self-concept. Someone else doesn't have that. They have a psyche built around thunderstorms, dogs that bite, and kittens that snuggle. Everyone has had different experiences, and therefore, everyone is building a different personal mind inside. No one is doing it purposely; it's reactive. It happens quite naturally because you're not ready to openly experience life. The highest state is to be comfortable learning and growing from life's experiences. But if you're not comfortable with some experiences, you use your will to resist them. That merely means you're not evolved enough in that area. There is physical evolution and there is spiritual evolution. They both involve adaptability to your environment. The former for your body, and the latter for "you" in there, the soul.

When events come in, they are meant to be experienced by you. If you have trouble experiencing them, that's the whole purpose of learning to accept. What right do you have to either cling to or resist reality? You didn't make reality, and you weren't here for the billions of years that created it. We're back to, "Do you like the fact that Saturn has rings?" Your answer was, "It's none of my business." That's the correct response for every bit of reality that took billions of years to end up in front of you.

The real question is not whether you like things, it's why are you not okay with them? The reason is actually quite simple: because you can't digest them. It's hard to let some experiences just pass through without residual disturbance. But you need to learn how to do it. You learned to play tennis. You learned to play the piano. You've learned all kinds of things, maybe even calculus. You didn't know how to do these things to start with. They were surely uncomfortable until you learned to be comfortable with them. The soul can learn. You in there, the consciousness, can learn to experience reality. In order to do so, you must not resist. Otherwise, you're going to immediately push reality away. That's what acceptance is: nonresistance. It is having the commitment to fully allow reality to pass directly into the highest part of your being. In the end, all you are surrendering is your resistance to reality. You learn to let it come in, even if it is not comfortable as it pours into you.

The same thing is true with positive experiences, like the butterfly. Somebody you like comes up to you and says, "You know, I really like you. You're very attractive to me, and I enjoy being with you." That is such a nice experience that you immediately cling to the beautiful things they said. They go back to what they were doing, but you can't. You can't focus on your work because the impressions left in your mind keep distracting you. This is the opposite of *Be Here Now;* you're practicing *Be There Then.* You just had a beautiful experience, and you ruined it. You ruined it by holding on to it, like the butterfly. You ruined it by creating a preference about one of life's experiences. Now every time the phone rings, and it's not the person who said the nice things, you get disappointed. Be aware that you did this. Somebody said something nice to you, and you couldn't handle it. You couldn't just let it be a nice experience. Instead, you clung to it in your mind, and it actually messed you up.

Whether you use your will to resist or cling, these leftover impressions will stay in your mind. You've now created an entire layer of mind that's holding your samskaras, your unfinished patterns from the past. You will come to see that these acts of clinging and resisting determine the quality of your life. These impressions distract your consciousness from the reality of the current moment. What is more, if you are constantly distracted by these samskaras in your mind, you're never going to experience who you really are.

There is a vast difference between memory and a samskara. Just as your computer has memory storage capability, so does your mind. It is a natural function of the mind to store compressed versions of what was received by the senses in its long-term memory. These stored memories can be retrieved with the slightest intent. You learn a person's name, meaning it is stored in long-term memory. When you see them again, the name normally comes up into the forefront of mind without any effort, though admittedly, sometimes we have to apply willful effort to bring the memory back. These are fairly normal ways memory is stored and recalled.

In drastic contrast to normal memory, if you experience an event that you have trouble handling when it renders in your mind, you use will to either consciously or subconsciously suppress it. You don't want it in your mind at all, not presently or long-term, so you try to push it out of the mind completely. When you do this, you are resisting the entire event: what came in through the senses, what you felt emotionally, and what your thoughts were about it. This resisted "package" of the experience cannot pass through you in the normal fashion—because you won't let it. The entire energy of the event is locked inside of your mind, and it does not sit there quietly. Because it keeps trying to release its blocked energies, it can distort your memories of the past as well as disturb your experience of the present. Blocked energies in the mind are like a computer virus that distorts both the conscious and subconscious minds. In later chapters we will deeply explore how these blocked energy patterns, samskaras, also block your natural energy flow.

When you commit to spiritual growth, you work on letting go of the stored blockages from the past and not storing any more from the present. This does not mean the mind's normal memory storage process does not take place. You are not willfully forgetting life's experiences. You are simply not resisting or clinging to the experiences, and thus not storing them as samskaras. They remain harmless, objective memories.

Let's take an example very close to home for some people. You have an ex-husband: "I don't want to see him. I don't want to talk about him ever again. I don't even like it when someone says his name. It makes me uncomfortable, even years after the divorce!" This is not objective memory talking—it is definitely a samskara. You say you divorced your ex-husband, but you really didn't. He's still inside bothering you. You don't even want to go to a party if you think he might be there. You have kept these impressions blocked in your mind, and ultimately you have created an alternate universe in which you are still dealing with your ex. Normal memory is not like this; it is well behaved. Like a computer's memory, it does not pop up by itself. It does not have blocked energies that need to be released. Normal memory is there when you need it—it does not haunt you throughout your life.

Fortunately, most things you encounter in life are neutral to you. They pass through unblocked and are available for recall when appropriate. You have driven by white lines on the road many times, but they don't come back up by themselves at inopportune times. Neither do the cars, trees, buildings, and myriad other objects you encounter each day. They come in, and they pass through. But there are a few things that are harder to deal with inside, and therefore you resist them or you cling to them. This is how you fell out of the garden of reality. Impressions stayed inside your mind and became the foundation blocks upon which you built your psyche.

CHAPTER 14

The Veil of the Psyche

Your psyche is like a computer program running in your mind based on your samskaras. It's in there talking to you about things that happened before, what you wish would happen now, and what you hope does or doesn't happen tomorrow. You've actually created an alternate reality inside your mind that is very complex. It's a tremendous menagerie of the stored moments you were not able to let go of. At this point, you don't even need another rattlesnake to get you disturbed. The fact that the experience of the snake is stuck in your mind means other things will remind you of it. In fact, you can remind yourself of it without the need of an external reminder. You're driving down the street, minding your own business. Suddenly, you remember how scary that snake was, and you get scared again. We're not dealing with reality anymore. We have such a mess built up in there that it's no wonder we have so much trouble with life. Such is the nature of the personal mind.

Regardless of how messy it gets in there, the fact remains that the personal mind is not you—no more than your TV screen is you. But it's much more difficult to objectively watch your mind than your TV screen. This is because of the power of the impressions you have stored in your mind. These past impressions compete with the image of reality coming in from the outside and make it hard to tell which is which. It is difficult to maintain a seat of objective observation when it gets so confusing in there. Samskaras are not to be taken lightly; they seriously distort your experience of life.

Let's take the example of a psychological Rorschach test, often referred to as an inkblot test. The psychologist holds up an inkblot and asks what you see. You immediately respond that you see people making love or, perhaps, mommy and daddy fighting. In other words, the Rorschach test stimulates the patterns you've stored inside your mind, causing you to see what's not actually there. The truth is the whole world is a giant Rorschach test. The world is a flow of atoms unfolding in front of you. It's no more personal than the inkblots. But it's hitting your samskaras, and that stimulates stored mental and emotional reactions. Now, instead of experiencing what is passing by outside, you are experiencing the likes, dislikes, beliefs, and judgments stored inside. These impressions are so strong that you actually think they are what is really out there, just like the inkblots. The personal mind has taken over your entire life. You are no longer free to enjoy the experiences that are actually happening—you are forced to deal with what your mind says is happening.

Let's look a little deeper into how samskaras affect your life. We have discussed that what is coming in from the outside stimulates your mental blockages from the past. Past experiences were uncomfortable when you first resisted them, and they are going to be uncomfortable when they come back up. To make matters worse, just as with the Rorschach test, you are not seeing what is actually outside—you are seeing your inner issues projected onto the outside. That's why life seems so scary and why it seems to always be hitting your weak spots. *The truth is, life is not hitting your weak spots, you are projecting your weak spots onto life.* Yet not everything you stored in there was negative. You held on to some positive things from the past. The problem is they're not happening anymore, and that is disappointing. If you go back to the same place where you saw the butterfly, and it's not there, it becomes a negative experience.

Understand, you have just made life a lose-lose situation. If anything reminds you of what bothered you before, you lose. If you are not getting to reexperience what you liked before, you lose. This is in drastic contrast to what Zen calls *beginner's mind*. If you are not expecting anything in particular from a situation, and then something special happens, it can touch you really deeply. It could be a beautiful sunset, the first unexpected kiss, or some other welcome surprise. If it touches you so deeply because you have no samskaras in your mind about the event—you have beginner's mind. Otherwise, you will be expecting something based on prior experiences, and that will interfere with the spontaneity of the event.

The end result is that these samskaras have ruined your life. You've made it so that unless something drastically different happens to pull you out of this preference system, you can't feel anything fully. That's why some people must go to the extremes to get a rush. It is also why some people try to keep everything exactly the same so life doesn't disturb their samskaras. In either case, trying to keep the mind a decent place to live in can force people to look for escapes, such as drinking and drugs. You get to the point where you're running around trying to appease your mind.

Eventually, you will come to realize that it's not the job, the spouse, or the car that gets old—it's listening to the mess in your mind that gets old. While all of these patterns from the past are blocked in your mind, you in there can neither experience the miracle of life unfolding before you, nor can you experience the natural beauty within you. Your awareness is completely distracted by these stored mental patterns, and you must devote your days and nights to serving them. You can no longer experience reality—you are stuck experiencing yourself.

There's a concept in Zen known as "just tree." It fits perfectly with our discussion. The story goes as follows: There was a young Buddhist monk in a monastery who would go for daily sessions with the Zen master. The master would ask him some questions, and the monk would leave. One time when the young monk walked in, the master looked at him and remarked, "What happened to you? You look so alive and filled with light."

The monk was surprised. "What do you mean?"

"I see a difference in you, my son. What happened?"

The monk told him, "I was walking across the courtyard and saw the big oak tree. I stopped and looked at it. I had seen it many times before, but this time I saw *just tree.* I just saw the tree. Somehow, it took me to such a deep place that I felt an awakening. I felt a moment of enlightenment. It took me beyond myself."

"That tree has been there for a hundred years," the master reflected. "You have walked by that tree every single day since you've been here."

"Yes," the student said, "but when I previously walked by the tree, it often reminded me of the tree Buddha sat under when he reached enlightenment. Other times, the tree reminded me of the one I fell out of when I was little. The tree always stimulated thought patterns from my past. This time I saw *just tree*."

The master smiled.

"Just tree" is what we talked about in the beginning of our discussion of mind. The tree comes in, renders in your mind, and that's all you see. In contrast, the tree comes in, renders in your mind, and stimulates any past samskaras you have about trees. Your samskara mind becomes activated, and your consciousness is scattered between the primary image of the tree and the secondary explosion that takes place inside. The secondary explosion is the reaction within your mind due to the stored patterns there. You can't have pure experiences anymore. The young monk did—he saw "just tree." If you didn't understand this before, hopefully you do now. A Zen master would be pleased with you, because "just tree" is a very deep concept in Zen Buddhism.

There is nothing wrong with the mind itself. Just like there is nothing wrong with a computer, per se. It is how you use these powerful gifts that can cause a problem. There is almost no limit to the brilliance of mind. People think Einstein was smart, but they don't understand their own brilliance. We all have the human mind, every single one of us. We don't have a possum mind, a squirrel mind, or even an ape mind. We have the human mind, and the human mind is brilliant.

CHAPTER 15

The Brilliant Human Mind

What's so special about the human mind? Let's take a look. For billions and billions of years, while the planet Earth was spinning through space, the process of evolution took place. There were minerals, then plants, then animals, all formed from atoms created in the stars. The planet had been floating in space for 4.5 billion years before modern humans showed up. It is worth noting that before humans showed up, life on Earth for the other species stayed pretty much the same. Food, shelter, and survival were the name of the game. Things haven't really changed that much for them. The monkeys lived in trees for tens of millions of years, just as they do now. The fish swam in the waters for hundreds of millions of years, just as they do now. Everything on Earth stayed pretty much the same until you humans showed up with your human mind. You discovered electricity and made the nighttime bright. You built giant skyscrapers and machinery that never existed before. You even dug into the earth, extracted minerals, and developed advanced materials like silicon chips. Then you built a rocket ship, got in, and flew to the moon.

Compare that to what any other animals have done. They are living exactly the same as they did a thousand years ago, a hundred thousand years ago, a million years ago. You're not. You used to live in caves; now you're planning to live on Mars. What did that? Did God hide a rocket ship, and you found it somewhere? No, your mind did that. Your mind figured out everything was made of atoms, then you figured out how split the atom. The human mind actually figured out how the universe was made, all the way down to the quantum level. Your mind put up the Hubble Space Telescope that can see back to the beginning of creation.

The Hubble can pick up light that has been traveling through space for more than thirteen billion years. This allows us to see what was happening thirteen billion years ago. Can you even think about that? The fact is you can because you have a human mind.

The human mind is an amazing thing. That is some serious stuff we've figured out. You're back in there, deep inside, and you have the use of a brilliant mind. That said, what is the average human doing with their mind? Einstein used his mind to ponder "thought experiments" about the behavior of light, gravity, and the physics of outer space (even though no human had ever been there!). Meanwhile, you keep your mind busy with relationships, what people think of you, and how to get what you want and avoid what you don't want. You may not have Einstein's mind, but compared to any other living thing on Earth, your mind is brilliant. The question is not whether your mind is brilliant; the question is what are you doing with that brilliance?

What we see so far is that the mind by itself, without you interfering, is doing what it's supposed to be doing. It's giving you the gift of rendering the outside world for you to experience. But you had some trouble accepting that gift. You started resisting when it felt a little too uncomfortable and clinging when it felt a little too good. This caused the buildup of mental patterns inside of you. Now, processing current external experiences becomes distorted by the reactions of past samskaras.

You can think of this as layers of the mind. The first layer is where the rendering of the present external experience is taking place. We can call that the *here-and-now layer.* The next layer is the stored patterns from the past that you did not release when the external experience was over. We can call that the *samskara layer.* But there is yet another layer. This layer is what you are doing with your brilliant mind to try to solve the discomforts created by the samskaras. This is the *personal-thoughts layer,* and it is the one you identify with the most—you think this is who you are. The combination of these three layers is what we call the *personal mind.* Yours is completely unique to you and you alone.

We create the personal-thoughts layer when we use the tremendous intellectual power of our mind to conceptualize an outside world that will not bother us and will, in fact, make us feel good. It seems perfectly logical. The problem is, what we think will make us feel good or bad is simply the result of blocked mental patterns from the past. If we use our mind's brilliance to develop thought patterns based on how everyone and everything needs to be for us to feel okay, we have limited our life to serving our samskaras. And our personal thoughts don't stop here. What good is it to analyze how you need things to be if you're not also going to think about how to get them that way? First we figure out the strategy of how to be okay, then we figure out the tactics of how to make it happen. Strategy and tactics—that's military training. In essence, we are at war with the world.

The personal mind has taken on the task of how to get the world unfolding in front of you to be the way you want. That should set off alarm bells because we've already discussed in great detail where the world in front of you comes from, and it has nothing to do with what's going on inside your head. The moment in front of you is the result of all the natural forces that caused it to be as it is. The preference system in your mind is the result of the past experiences that you couldn't handle. These are two totally different sets of forces that have nothing to do with each other. For example, there are current impersonal forces that are causing it to rain. There are past personal forces causing you to not like the rain. You have just pitted yourself against the universe, and you are going to lose. Nevertheless, the personal mind thinks it's right. You actually think that the universe should be the way you want it to be.

PART IV

Thoughts and Dreams

CHAPTER 16

The Abstract Mind

Fortunately, your mind has a layer beyond the layers of the personal mind. It has been called the impersonal mind, the abstract mind, or even the purely intellectual mind. This layer of mind is not distracted by the inner commotion caused by your samskaras. It is free to soar unhindered into the pure brilliance and creativity of a higher expression of mind.

This higher layer of your mind, which we will call the *abstract layer,* is what allows you to build rocket ships, develop air-conditioning, and discover the existence of atoms. The abstract mind is what truly makes humans great. You are not limited to experiencing only through your senses; you are free to explore in the realm of pure intellectual mind. Your mind can take you pretty much anywhere. Do you want to build rovers that can go to Mars so you can explore the planet on the internet? Wonderful, you can do that because your mind is capable of expanding beyond the limit of your senses and the limit of your personal thoughts. Mind can operate at many levels—the question is, what are you doing with it?

Intellectually, you have the ability to take images from outside and do creative things with them. You are free to use your mind's power to be artistically abstract and intellectually logical. A perfect example of the latter would be Einstein's thought experiments. Einstein came up with many of his greatest theories sitting in his armchair and reasoning out very abstract concepts. This is a great tribute to the power of our minds. It is a far cry from getting lost in your personal thoughts and making these thoughts about yourself the total meaning of your life. Once you create thoughts about what you want and don't want, and how to force the world to be that way, you will never be okay inside. You will lose much of the great power of abstract thought because you cannot abstract from yourself. Life will become a battle between reality and your mental preferences. This use of mind is called the personal mind because its thoughts are all about you and your concepts, views, and preferences.

The teachings of mindfulness, which center awareness on the current moment, encourage you to focus on something other than the personal mind. Focusing on the moment is one way to get your consciousness off its incessant addiction to the personal. Another way to transcend the personal mind is by using your intellectual mind to create and do things that are not personal in nature. This includes being an engineer who reasons out problems or a medical researcher who studies diseases and how to cure them. Artistry, computer science, mathematics—all of these are examples of beautiful uses of the impersonal mind. The mind is great; it's just not supposed to be used for storing all your personal preferences and then thinking the whole world is supposed to match what you stored.

The outside world is simply not going to magically match what you've stored in your mind. In fact, it is not very intelligent to expect it to. Is it really intelligent to devote your life to fighting with life so it aligns with your past good and bad experiences? How can you enjoy life if you are always worrying and struggling to get it your way? That's what all of our societies are doing, and that's what almost every human being has done. People just haven't evolved enough to learn not to do that. Rich people, poor people, sick people, healthy people, married people, single people—they all are bound in the same way. If they get what they want, they are relatively okay. If they don't get what they want, they suffer to a greater or lesser extent. Fortunately, you do not have to live this way. There is a much higher way to live life. But it requires that you change how you interact with your mind and with the life unfolding before you.

To understand this transformation, let's first take a look at how you even decided what you want and don't want. If you pay attention, you will see that your past experiences determine your preferences. You didn't just make it all up from scratch—your views, opinions, and preferences are formulated based on data from your past. For example, let's say you are totally secure in your love relationship until you hear that your friends had a breakup, and they are miserable. All of a sudden you start worrying about your own relationship. You were fine before you heard about your friends, but now you're not. You stored the concept of a breakup inside your mind, even though it really had nothing to do with you. You took it personally.

Is it possible to process the information without it getting stuck in your mind? Of course it is. Your friends had a problem, and they shared it with you. It came into your mind, passed through your consciousness, and you experienced the feeling of compassion. The interaction actually made you a greater being. You were able to fully absorb the reality of life without it getting stuck in your mind. If you want to recall it later, you can willfully restore it from memory in all its glory. But it will not keep coming back up by itself. Since it did not get stuck in the conscious mind, or shoved into the subconscious, it will not adversely affect your life. It actually made you a better person because you were able to handle the experience.

On the other hand, if you were not able to process the experience without resisting it, it will stay stuck in the conscious mind and create havoc. If you really resist it, it will get shoved down into the subconscious where it will fester and spread its disturbance throughout the mind. In either case, you are storing what you are afraid of in your mind. If you do this, you will be afraid of your own thoughts. How could you not be? You made a collection of unpleasant thoughts in your mind, and they are going to keep coming back up. Now, in order to live in there, the analytical aspect of mind must be utilized to figure out what needs to happen outside for you to be okay. This is where preferences come from. They are simply attempts to use outside events to solve the fact that you are not doing well inside. This results in the constant practice of judging everything that's unfolding based on your preferences.

It's easy to see why people don't agree with each other. Nobody else has had the experiences that came in through your eyes. What you have inside your mind is completely different from what others have inside their minds. It can't be otherwise because the data in your mind came from the experiences you had. Nobody else had those experiences, not even close—not your spouse, your children, or your friends. Not only were your past experiences different, but you processed them differently. We can certainly force ourselves to conform to other ways of thinking in order to gain acceptance, but that just makes living inside all the more complicated. You not only have your default way of thinking resulting from your stored past impressions, but now you must suppress parts of that in order to conform to the "group" mindset. No wonder it gets messy in there!

You are holding all that personal stuff inside your mind—the good, the bad, and the ugly. The inevitable result is that if the moment in front of you happens to align well with your stored patterns, you feel great. You feel open, excited, and enthused. If it doesn't align well with your stored patterns, you get upset. You immediately close, get defensive, and maybe even get depressed. Now we're back to the question we asked earlier, "What's it like living in there?" Sometimes it's nice; sometimes it's not. Sometimes it's heaven; sometimes it's hell. This is why. It is not because God made it that way. You did this. You were given free will, and what you did with your free will was make a mess out of your mind. Instead of being in awe that the moment in front of you even exists, you fight with it to make it match what you want.

CHAPTER 17

Serve Mind or Fix It

All your preferences exist because you stored experiences from the past inside your personal mind. This makes it difficult to live in there, but instead of fixing it, you double down and try to satisfy your preferences. "I want to feel good, and the way to feel good is by getting the house I want." "The way to feel good is by owning the car I've always wanted." "The way to feel good is by finding a better relationship—this one's not doing it for me." These attempts to compensate for your blockages are, at best, short lived because you are not actually getting rid of the blockages.

The foundational choice we have in life is either constantly control life to compensate for our blockages or devote our lives to getting rid of our blockages. The fact is we stored these samskaras inside. We shouldn't have, but we did. Now instead of getting rid of them, we expect the world to adapt to them. We know it's not going to happen by itself, so we use the personal-thoughts layer of mind to analyze how the world needs to be to match what we want. We're brilliant at figuring out how to make someone become attracted to us, or to change things so they better fit our limitations. Almost everything we do is governed by this personal-thoughts layer of mind. It is the same analytical power of mind that Einstein used to see $E = mc^2$, but you're using it to figure out what to do if someone's talking badly about you. This entire layer of mind intellectualizes and analyzes your stored patterns to try to figure out how the world needs to be so that when it comes in, it will feel good and never feel bad.

That is why you tend to have so much trouble making decisions. You're trying to figure out how each choice will make you feel later.

"Where do I want to live? Should I change jobs? I need to figure this out." You're trying to mentally conceptualize how the proposed action will match the patterns you've stored inside. You don't even think twice about it. "Of course that's what I'm doing. What else would I do?" How about live in reality and enjoy the moments that are unfolding in front of you? That's what else you can do. Use your mind to be creative, inspiring, and do great things. Don't let the mind always be thinking about itself and what it wants. Learn to enjoy life as it is—instead of limiting the ways you can enjoy it to serve your past impressions.

The self-centered, analyzing layer of mind is the worst. It is the model you build about how everything and everybody needs to be for you to feel okay, including the weather tomorrow. "It better not rain tomorrow, I'm going camping." Now you're getting upset about the weather! You have no control over the weather, yet it's bothering you. It's not just the weather. The driver in front of you is going ten miles per hour below the speed limit. Let's watch your mind: "This is ridiculous. I don't have time for this. What's wrong with them? They're supposed to be in the slow lane." Turns out the problem is not how the person in front of you is driving. The problem is what your mind is doing about how the person in front of you is driving. Eventually you catch on that you've developed an entire intellectual model of how every single thing needs to be: how people should behave, how your spouse should be dressed when you're going out, even how much traffic there should be. How many things do you do this about? Pretty much every single thing. You honestly believe that what you made up is how it should be. The truth of the matter is, that's absurd. There is no way what you made up in your head, based upon your very limited past experiences, has anything to do with what's supposed to be happening in the real world.

Think about it for a moment. What you want the weather to be has nothing to do with what it's going to be. The weather has to do with meteorology, not your preference system. If you really want to know why it had to rain on your day off, go study science. A wise person realizes that the world is not going to unfold the way they want it to because it's not supposed to. No two of us agree how it's supposed to unfold, yet there's only one world out there. We best leave reality to either science or God, not to everyone's individual preferences. The world in front of you has the power of reality behind it. It is unfolding in accordance to the influences that made it be the way it is, and there are billions of influences going back billions of years. In contrast, you're just making up how it's supposed to be based on the impressions you held inside from your past. When reality doesn't happen the way you want, you say reality is wrong. "I don't like that. It should not have happened."

Here's a technique for getting perspective. Put your mind in outer space and realize that there's nothing out there but 99.999 percent emptiness. There's just empty space between all the stars. Your nearest star after the Sun is 4.2 light-years away. To get an idea of how far that is, imagine holding a light beam above the Earth. Now, let it go for one second. In that one second the light circumnavigated the globe seven and a half times. Travel at that speed every second for 4.2 years, and you'll reach the next star. There's pretty much nothing but empty space in between. We call it interstellar space. That's how it is between all the stars, all over the universe. How would you like to be out there and see nothing? Because that's what 99.999 percent of the universe is. What you get every day is a miracle! There are colors, shapes, and sounds along with all the amazing experiences you're given with each passing moment. Yet all you do is say, "No, it's not what I want." Of course it's not what you want. That's not the point. Instead of comparing the moment in front of you against the preferences you've built up inside your mind, why don't you compare it against nothing? Since that's what makes up 99.999 percent of the universe.

If you do this, you'll find yourself being thankful that you get to have your daily experiences. They are certainly better than empty space. That's how a wise person lives. The alternative is to suffer because things are not the way you want. Previously, we discussed Buddha's first noble truth: *All of life is suffering.* Now we get to the second noble truth: *The cause of suffering is desire.* In other words, the cause of suffering is preference, deciding how you want things to be and getting upset when they're not that way. Not surprisingly, it turns out Buddha was right. Events don't cause mental or emotional suffering—you cause yourself mental and emotional suffering about the events. If you are not doing that, things are the way they are. Always remember, it took 13.8 billion years of everything unfolding exactly as it did for the moment in front of you to be the way it is.

A perfect example of how we cause ourselves mental suffering is how we view our bodies. When you're young, you look a certain way. You get older, and you look another way. What's wrong with that? It's just miraculous. You watch your body change all by itself. That is a natural process, and it should not cause suffering. Likewise, in this life you go through many different experiences. They should not cause suffering. Experiences are not suffering. They are experiences. But if you decide how you want them to be, and they're not that way, then you suffer. *Suffering is caused by the contrast between what you mentally decided you wanted and the reality unfolding in front of you.* To whatever degree they don't match, you suffer.

What we're exploring here is deeper than most people want to go, but it is the truth. You have set up in your mind what you like and what you don't like based on your past impressions. Now you honestly believe the world should be that way. Obviously, that's not a belief founded in reality. As long as you do that, you're going to have a very hard time in life.

We now have a pretty clear view of the personal mind. We have seen that the first layer of mind is the one that receives the senses. The second layer is the samskaras we did not let pass through as life flowed into us. Based on this foundation, we built very personal thought patterns of like and dislike and how to get life to unfold the way we want. These impressions of what we liked and disliked are so powerful that our consciousness becomes completely absorbed in the model of life they generate. In fact, we focus on it so completely that it forms our self-concept. "I am the one who likes this, doesn't like that, and I'm dead serious about getting what I want." We are so distracted by this model that we're not even aware of being back there watching all this. But we are—how else would we know it's going on?

CHAPTER 18

Willful and
Automatic Thoughts

You're in there, and you have the ability to create a thought. Right now say "Hello" inside your head. Say it over and over again. It's doing it, isn't it? If you had not purposely said that word, it would not have been in your mind, would it? You clearly have the ability to willfully make your mind create thoughts. In general, there are two very distinct types of thoughts: willful and automatic. The first one we'll explore, as its name indicates, is a thought that you willfully create.

You can willfully create thoughts in two different ways. You can create auditory thoughts through the voice inside your head talking to you, saying "Hello," or you can create visualizations in your mind's eye. For example, right now, visualize a boat. Do you see it in your mind? Now visualize a bigger boat, and an even bigger one. See the *Queen Mary* in there. That boat would not be in there unless you purposely willed it to be. Once again, we see that you clearly have the ability to make your mind create thoughts.

There's another category of thoughts besides willful thoughts: automatic thoughts. These are the thoughts you did not purposely decide to create—they just pop into your mind on their own. You may pay attention to them once they're there, but you did not willfully decide to create them like you did with the boat. The vast majority of your thoughts are automatically generated. You're driving down the street enjoying your day, and your mind starts creating thoughts by itself: "Why did I have to say those things? If I hadn't said them, we might still be together. Well, that's unlikely—we were having problems before that." You're not willfully making your mind create these thoughts. This is that voice inside your head talking on its own. If you doubt that this is happening by itself, try stopping it for any length of time. The mind's stream of thoughts will return in no time.

Let's say somebody was supposed to call you at three o'clock and by three thirty they still haven't called. What happens during those thirty minutes? Your mind creates thoughts by itself. You are not willfully deciding, "I want to worry about this. Okay, mind, start creating worrisome thoughts. Did he have an accident or is he standing me up?" You're not doing that. Your mind is doing it all by itself. They're not even meaningful thoughts—they're destructive thoughts. They are ruining your thirty minutes. The question becomes, if you're going to end up waiting thirty minutes for the person to call, why do you want to make yourself miserable? Well, technically, you're not. Your mind is doing it for you.

If you pay attention, you will see that the mind creates most thoughts on its own. They go on all the time. Just watch yourself in the shower. Watch yourself when you're driving. Watch yourself whenever you take a break from work. You'll see the mind is constantly creating thoughts. Even when someone is talking to you, the words may be coming in through your senses, but you're not totally listening to them. You're also listening to your mind's reaction to what's being said. You're thinking, "I don't agree with that. I would never do it that way." Your mind just made the discussion all about you instead of what the person is saying. If you watch those automatically generated thoughts, you'll see they range anywhere from funny to frightening. Regardless, is it so smart to have all that noise going on inside your head all the time? If you bother to pay attention to it, you're going to find out that it's not.

Where do those thoughts come from? Why does the mind create thoughts by itself without you willfully doing it? We've actually already discussed this. When you store a samskara, an unfinished mental and emotional pattern, that pattern will not sit quietly inside of you. Anything that ever got stored inside your mind, because you resisted or clung to it, is trying to release. It's an energetic reality, like Newton's laws of motion. The energy cannot stay in there unless you continuously assert an opposing force of will to keep it in there. That's why it keeps coming back up. Mommy yelled at you twenty-five years ago, and that hurt you. Now suddenly somebody mentions their mother yelling and all these emotional and mental issues come up inside of you. Why? That blocked energy is always trying to come up, every single millisecond. Just like in a dammed-up river, the blockage is trying to release its pent-up energy. It is not comfortable staying inside you, so you have to constantly assert your willpower to hold it down. How much energy are you wasting keeping all this garbage inside?

Just as your body is always trying to expel impurities, so your mind is trying to get these mental impurities out. That is what's happening when your mind creates its own thoughts. Sometimes you will be able to trace those thoughts back to their source; other times it's not so easy. The important thing to realize is there's always a reason why your mind creates one thought versus another.

Let's go back to the example of someone being late with a phone call. Your mind could begin creating worrisome thoughts about what you might have done to upset them so much that they aren't calling. But that is not the meaningful question. The meaningful question is, why did that possible reason come up versus any other? Turns out, when you were ten years old, somebody once said, "You're right, I didn't call you. It was on purpose because I didn't like what you did." Now years later, when somebody doesn't call, that comes back up. What if years ago when a person didn't call, the reason was they wanted to surprise you by personally coming by with a special gift. Now when someone doesn't call, you feel all excited about what might happen next. These impressions get left inside you. They will continuously try to release pent-up energy, and they will end up determining the thoughts your mind creates on its own. This is the nature of almost all your automatic thoughts. They are not to be seen as some important truth or great insight into what is really going on. They are simply your mind attempting to cleanse the patterns you have stored in there.

CHAPTER 19

Dreams and the Subconscious

To get a better understanding of how stored mental energies get released, let's turn to a favorite topic of psychology: dreams. What are dreams? The traditional Freudian concept of dreams is that some events happening outside leave unfinished impressions in the mind. A little boy wants a bicycle but doesn't get one. He goes to sleep and dreams he's got a bicycle. The original bicycle event didn't sit well, so the boy pushed it away in his mind. He suppressed it. When he went to sleep and was not controlling his thoughts as much, the mind was free to release what it had not been free to express while the boy was awake. We all experience this type of dream fairly regularly. A charged event from the waking world finds its way into our dream world. You are not willfully doing this. It is the mind trying to release built-up energy patterns.

There are all kinds of dreams. Freud called the dream we've been discussing basic *wish fulfillment*. It is a samskara formed in the waking mind releasing energy by creating the thoughts you watch while you're asleep. These thoughts that make up your dreams are not that different from the automatic thoughts going on in your waking mind. They are certainly much more vivid, especially in their imagery. This is because when you're sleeping, the mind can focus completely on creating the thoughts. It is not busy being distracted by the senses or the many other layers of thoughts and emotions going on. In addition, you're not willfully pushing the thoughts away. This is why the mind is much more creative when you fall asleep. It can create an entire, complex world in full 3D and Technicolor. Most people can't do that when they're awake, though obviously, their minds are perfectly capable of doing so.

Once you stop suppressing uncomfortable experiences, one thing you're going to realize is that there really is no subconscious mind, per se. The conscious mind and the subconscious mind are actually the same one mind, and the only reason we see a difference is because we artificially created a division. To understand this, imagine looking around a room of people and saying, "The people on the right side of the room I like; I'm comfortable with those people. The people on the left side of the room, however, I'm very uncomfortable with them." Having stated this, imagine you never again look at the left side of the room because it makes you uncomfortable. What you've just done is separated the room into the part you're comfortable with and the part you don't want anything to do with. The latter part exists, but no longer exists for you. That is exactly what you've done to create the subconscious mind. The part of your mind you're not willing to look at is what we call the subconscious.

Fortunately, these artificially divided parts of your mind will merge once you stop suppressing. You will get the rest of your mind back, and you will be able to use its full power. Imagine how much mental power you waste by pushing all that mess into the subconscious. Then you have to keep it down there for the rest of your life. It's really amazing what a mess we make because we can't handle the moments passing in front of us.

The thoughts we push down into the subconscious play a role in both our waking and dreaming states. The reason your mind is creating your automatically generated dream thoughts is the same reason your mind creates your automatically generated waking thoughts. In both cases, you are not willfully creating this mental activity. It is happening on its own as part of the mind's attempt to release blocked energies.

The common thread between your waking and dreaming states is that it's the same consciousness that is aware of both. You who is watching the dream is the same you who watches your waking thoughts and experiences the outside world. This is why when you wake up, you can say, "What a dream I had." How do you know? You know because you were there—the same you who is aware while you're awake. Interestingly, because it is the same you, there can be a lot of spiritual growth in dreams. Meher Baba, another great yoga master, said that you can work off karma in your dreams. He said that by going through an experience in your dreams, it is actually beneficial to your spiritual evolution. You're at least allowing some blocked energy to release that you didn't allow while you were awake, and that is healthy.

There is a great deal we can learn about ourselves from the dream state. If what you stored in the subconscious was more traumatic than simply not liking what happened or not getting what you wanted, what happens? Some things are much harder to deal with than just preferences. There are samskaras that are so deep they can't even come up in a dream. If they tried to release, you would wake from a nightmare in a very disturbed state. In other words, your consciousness isn't able to experience the event even when it manifests in a dream. You resist and become so uncomfortable about it that you wake up. So how does this energy release?

Unfinished energy stored in your mind is always trying to release at one level or another. If the release would wake you from a dream, your mind, all by itself, symbolizes what it's trying to express. Instead of dreaming about the car accident that killed your younger brother, you dream that there are birds flying high overhead and an eagle swoops down and takes one of the small birds away. You're willing to watch that, but you're not willing to watch a car accident with someone you love dying. This is all very real. Your mind is doing you a favor. Your brilliant mind did that in an attempt to stay healthy and release at least some of the pent-up energy. That's what the symbology of dreams is about. It's truly amazing how brilliant your mind is when left to its own resourcefulness. Just as your body is always trying to heal itself, so your mind is always trying to release these impurities that are stuck in there.

CHAPTER 20

Waking Dreams

At this point you can certainly appreciate the tremendous power of your mind, especially in regard to creating dreams on its own. Creating dreams is not a willful act; your mind has the power to do it by itself. But as you've seen, your dreams are not the only mental objects that your mind creates automatically. The voice inside your head that talks all day is the exact same expressive power of mind that creates your dreams. It would not be incorrect to call that dialog in your head your *waking dreams*. Every personal thing that voice says is because of the samskaras you have stored inside. Your mind is trying to release those blockages during the day while you're still awake. For example, you see somebody running and that voice says inside, "I wonder what he did wrong? It's like my brother when he ran away. What is this guy running away from?" The problem is that this current situation has nothing to do with your brother, and this person could be running for exercise. Your mind is using this opportunity to release energies that are pent up inside. That's why so much of the mind's dialog is negative. The vast majority of energy you have stored inside is because of things you didn't like. When subsequent events happen that stimulate these negative samskaras, the new events are automatically experienced as negative. In essence, the negativity keeps compounding.

If you really want to see how your preferences manage to make life a negative experience, go build a house and decide to paint the kitchen walls white. Do you know there are more than fifty shades of white? Just wait until you try to pick which white you want. In other words, there is only one tiny window of color choice that will align with your preferences and make you happy. All the rest will get you upset. Just look at the odds you're up against. There are billions of things that can happen in life that don't match your preferences, and there are only a few that do. Under these conditions, the probability that life is going to be a negative experience is extremely high. This is not because life is negative. It is because the only thing that isn't negative to you is that which exactly matches your preferences.

It is so important to understand this. You have set up a system in which you can't win. You have expanded what can bother you to include all experiences that remind you of what bothered you before. What is more, life almost never totally satisfies you because everything has to be exactly what you want—to a T. This shows you the power of past and present preferences—the more preferences you have, the less you will be okay.

So far, we've learned a lot about mind. We began with an understanding of empty mind. Then we discussed the here-and-now layer of mind, which internally renders the images being received by the senses. On top of that layer of mind, the real trouble begins. You in there, the conscious entity that knows you're there, used the power of will to keep certain images from passing right through. This resulted in the layer of mind called the samskara layer. It holds the impressions you stored from your past that are the basis for your personal preferences. As if it's not enough that you built this entire structure in your mind, you then committed your life to thinking about how to serve it. Your consciousness is pretty lost, constantly focusing on this false mental concept of self.

Fortunately, there is a way out—it's called *witness consciousness*. If you can learn to sit back and simply watch that voice inside your head, you can free yourself. This is not about shutting up the voice. Don't ever fight with your mind. You're the one who did this to your mind; how dare you complain about the mind. If you keep eating food that's making you sick, do you yell at the food? Of course not—you change your behavior. Likewise, since it is these stored samskaras that are messing up the greatness of your mind, you change your inner behavior. The way to do this is quite simple: release the samskaras you've already stored and don't store any more. Easier said than done, but we will certainly explore how to do this.

One thing complicates our task. The mind is not the only force making it difficult to find peace inside—there are also emotions. It's bad enough that the mind is constantly releasing stored energy through that inner voice, but the mind has a little sister, the heart. The heart can create emotions that make it really interesting to live in there. Sometimes it's like there are volcanos going on inside, and other times your inner state is so beautiful you just want to melt into it. What's going on with that? And more importantly, what can you do about it? As you might expect, that is exactly where we're going as we continue our journey into exploring what it's like to live inside yourself.

PART V

The Heart

CHAPTER 21

Understanding Emotions

Examining the nature of the world around us, as well as the nature of mind, teaches us a lot about ourselves. One thing becomes pretty clear: it's not always easy living inside. The thoughts being created by the mind can be very uncomfortable, and the world coming in through the senses can start a veritable firestorm within. On top of all this, there is something else we experience inside that can be even more disturbing than thoughts: emotions.

Emotions are very different from thoughts, but most people don't bother to separate them. The combination of your thoughts and emotions makes up what can be called your *psyche*, or your personal self. The psyche is completely distinct from your physical body. The psyche is the nonphysical world going on inside you.

Clearly seeing the difference between your thoughts and your emotions is very important. If you were asked to point to your thoughts, you would not point to your toes; you would point to the area around your head. This is because thoughts are generated in the mind which is associated with the brain. On the other hand, if you were asked to point to where emotions like love come from, you would point to your heart. That's why valentine cards have hearts on them and not toes—we associate the emotion of love with our heart. That is understandable because emotions are generated by the heart. Not just nice emotions—all emotions. If someone does something that hurts you or makes you jealous, you feel the pain or turmoil in your heart. If you get inspired at work, you can put your whole heart into the project. This is not referring to your physical heart— you can't put that into the project. What we are referring to is your spiritual heart or your energy heart, which we will soon discuss in great depth.

Your emotions are not physical. You can be standing next to someone who is experiencing joy or sadness, and they don't necessarily show it. Emotions are not something you see; they are something you feel. In fact, the words "emotions" and "feelings" are interchangeable. Just like you experience your thoughts inside, you experience your feelings inside. Nonetheless, your emotions are completely different from your thoughts.

Let's examine this difference. As we previously explored, your mind creates thoughts and presents them to you in two different ways. One is verbally via that voice inside your head, and the other is visually in your mind's eye. Your heart communicates quite differently. Your emotions do not talk to you verbally. They are not simply a voice inside your head saying, "I feel so jealous." The voice says that because you *feel* jealous. There is a feeling, a sensation—that is what an emotion is. That's why we use the word "feelings" when we talk about our emotions, as in "He hurt my feelings." Saying this means the interaction with the person created an emotion inside of you that was uncomfortable. Thus, you have verbal or visual thoughts inside your mind, and you also have these totally different things called emotions emanating from your heart. They are actually vibrations. They don't form specific objects like thoughts do. They're more etheric. Emotions are more like clouds instead of defined objects. They come up and can be like waves flowing over you. They flush what we call your *aura* or energy body. Emotions are simply the sensation of experiencing a change in your energy. Like Obi-Wan in *Star Wars* put it, "I felt a great disturbance in the Force."

You are always having inner feelings, but you don't notice them until they change. Notice that you only talk about emotions when they go to the extremes. "It hurt me tremendously. I can't believe how you hurt me." Or, "I felt so much love. It was the most beautiful feeling I ever had." These are examples of extremes in your emotions, and they catch your attention. You probably don't notice it, but you have a normal state of emotional energy flowing through your heart all day. When it drops out, you notice the change and say, "My heart fell out from under me. I lost my strength." Your heart can fall out from under you when fear takes over. Something happens and the energy just drops. In contrast, you can say, "My heart has wings." All of a sudden the emotional energy in your heart rises up and inspires you. These are changes from the steady state of emotional energy that normally flows through your heart. As you get more and more in tune with your emotions, you will notice that, like thoughts, emotions are almost always there.

Just as with thoughts, the questions become: Who is it that feels these emotional shifts? How do you know you feel anger? How do you know you feel love? You know because you are in there, and you are aware of what is going on in there. That clarity is very deep, spiritually. You have been so concerned about the emotions, themselves, you didn't realize you are the one in there experiencing them. The goal of this journey we are taking together is not to change your thoughts or emotions, it is for you to stay seated in the seat of Self while accepting these different shifts that are taking place. From this vantage point, the emotions can change, you can notice them changing, but you don't go anywhere. You remain the one who notices the emotions, hears the thoughts, and looks out through the eyes. Who is this one? This is what our journey is about. There is no spirituality anywhere except in the seat of Self. Spirituality is about spirit, and the seat of Self is spirit.

When you sit back in the seat of witness consciousness, it does not require a willful process of watching your emotions. Instead, it's the simple awareness of what is going on in there. It doesn't take will or effort to do this. You are simply aware that you hear or see your thoughts and that you feel your emotions. If you pay attention, you will notice emotions can be like the sensation of wind flowing over you. Wind can be very comfortable, like a gentle breeze. Or wind can be frightening, like a one hundred mile per hour hurricane blowing in your face. Surely you have noticed that emotions can be like this. It doesn't take effort to notice them, but it can take effort to handle what you notice. Emotions are very sensitive vibrations emanating from the heart, and as such they can shift very easily. The heart is much more sensitive than the mind, and we have much less control over it.

Without question, when your heart emanates a particular vibration of energy, your mind will start talking accordingly. It's very much like a freshwater spring. If you dive down to the source of the spring, there's going to be water bubbling up from the opening. When that water hits the surface, it creates ripples and all kinds of patterns. The activity on the surface is very different from what emanates at the source. So it is with your heart. Your heart is releasing energy of a given vibration rate, and that vibration rises into your mind automatically. You don't have to first notice that you feel jealous and then decide you had better think about it. What's going on in the heart ends up in the mind as thoughts. The samskaras you stored are trying to release their energy from the heart, and that is causing the mind to get active. The roots of the samskaras are stored in your heart. That is where the patterns you shoved out of your mind went. They did not dissipate. They went down further into the source of your energy flow, which is in your heart.

Very few people understand their heart. Many intellectuals just want to keep it suppressed because it is much too sensitive and reactive. They would rather live in the mind because they have more control there. Somebody hurts you, you feel an uncomfortable emotion, and you go right to the mind and rationalize it away: "He didn't mean it, it's okay. Don't take it so personally." That's if you're being positive. Otherwise, the negative mind starts in, "I'm not going to put up with this. Nobody is going to talk to me that way. Who do they think they are?" Either way, your mind is telling your heart, "It's okay, I'll take care of it." You're simply directing your awareness to your mind, so you don't have to feel the difficult emotions emanating from your heart.

Notice that consciousness can focus fully on the heart, fully on the mind, or it can divide its awareness between the two. When emotions are extremely pleasant, you may have the tendency to behave irrationally because you don't want to shift awareness from the beauty in your heart to the rational mind. On the other hand, when the emotions are unpleasant, you may try to change the inner experience by letting your thoughts distract you from what's happening in the heart. *The mind becomes a place the soul goes to hide from the heart.* To transcend this tendency to hide in either your heart or your mind, simply realize that it is always the same conscious awareness experiencing what is going on inside.

CHAPTER 22

Why the Heart Opens
and Closes

If you want to know your heart, first and foremost understand that you are not your heart—you are the experiencer of your heart. You are the consciousness that is aware when emotions are taking place. When love shoots up inside of you, and you say you're in love, what you really mean is that you feel love coming up from your heart and bathing you. You're floating in the ocean of love, but you're not the love you feel—you are the experiencer of the love you feel. Note that so far we haven't considered the role of another person in this love experience. This is because what's actually happening when you begin to feel love is your heart is opening and emanating a beautiful flow of energy. This should drive you to say, "I love love," but instead you say, "I love you." That is your first clue into the role of another person in your experience of love. As long as the other person's presence helps your heart open, you feel love for them. If their presence stops opening your heart, you start looking elsewhere. This is why human relationships are so difficult. We project the source of love outside, instead of realizing it is always inside.

The actual flow of love has to do with you and your heart. It has nothing to do with anybody else. It is an energy flow coming through your heart that you experience inside. Undoubtedly, certain people or circumstances can cause your heart to open or close. But the action of opening and closing is something your heart is doing, not the other person. By the time we're done with this discussion, you will understand why this happens. For now, let's look at what happens if we don't under-stand that love is a totally inner experience and we project that experience onto someone else.

The moment we project the source of love outside ourselves, every-thing becomes personal. We tend to become possessive, and that is only natural. We want to feel love and have projected the experience onto another person. To keep feeling the love, we have to keep the other person. The very human emotions of jealously, need, and dependency result from this. Likewise, if we are feeling the flow of love and our lover does some-thing we don't like, we feel closed and hurt. These are just other feelings that can emanate from the heart.

If you want to continue feeling love, you have to learn how to deal with emotions that open and close the heart. It's like learning to play an instrument. At first, you don't know how to do it. You're going to make mistakes and learn from the experience. The heart is a very sophisticated instrument·that few people know how to play. If the heart opens, they try to possess the things that helped it open. If the heart closes, they try to protect themselves from the things that caused it to close. Since you have to live with the consequences of your actions, it can be life changing to understand why the heart opens and closes, and who it is that notices.

You do notice that your heart opens and closes, right? Regardless of whether a person has studied yoga, or ever meditated in their life, every-one understands the heart can open and close. When the heart is open, you experience a more uplifted state than at other times. When the heart is closed, it's very difficult and painful to live with. Unfortunately, most people don't have the slightest idea what's going on when this happens. If they were told right now to open their heart, they wouldn't know what to do. They know how to clench their fist, blink their eyes, and even create a thought—but they don't know how to willfully open their heart. Generally, the heart opens and closes on its own, and people just have to live with the consequences.

Better be careful about your heart. You can get so involved in the initial rush of energy when it opens that you get carried away. People have been known to say, "I'm totally blown away. I'm so in love. I don't care where I live. I'll live outside in a tent as long as I'm with them." Let's see how long that lasts. When the heart closes, it becomes, "I don't ever want to see them again. I don't care what they say. I don't even want to talk to them. I can't believe they did that." If you get lost listening to the closed heart express itself, you might not want to see where you end up.

Your heart is a thing, like an appliance. It's an appliance that emanates vibrations of energies. Like an appliance, it needs a healthy power source. When the heart is closed, you don't feel positive energies or a constructive purpose. It can get pretty hard and uncomfortable in there. Sometimes it feels like a rock inside your chest. You definitely don't want that, so in an attempt to avoid the experience, your mind starts making up stories of what to do. "I'm going to leave them. They'll be so sorry." Can we talk honestly about this? The generation of these thoughts is just a process that happens in the psyche. When the heart closes, the energy flow is not strong, and this results in negative thoughts. It takes energy to raise things, and that includes the level of your thoughts. When the heart is closed for a period of time, people can even go into deep depression. That doesn't happen when the heart is open. Note that whatever state the heart is in, it feels like it's going to stay that way. Yet, you've seen at different points of your life that the heart does change if given the chance. People get so lost in the experience of the blocked heart that they ruin their lives over it. What the mind says when the heart is closed is not you. It's just the mind expressing the state of the closed heart. You are the one who notices.

What if your heart is in an excited, open state? You're just as dangerous because you think it's not going to change. Generally, something is going to happen that curbs the enthusiasm pouring through your heart. If there is a reason that the heart opened, then there is a reason it can close. The world keeps changing; your mind keeps changing; everything keeps changing. Therefore, if you can point to a reason why your heart is open, be careful—it will change. If you can point to a reason why your heart is closed, don't worry—it will change. If you let it, your heart will go through fluctuations as different situations cause it to open and close. When you don't understand this, you just react to your heart. It takes a truly great being to understand the heart. This is because they have spent years objectively observing the heart's behavior rather than running after what it wants or running away from what it doesn't want.

A very important aspect of spiritual growth is understanding the dynamics of the opening and closing of the heart. In order to fully explore why the heart opens and closes, we must first bring our discussion to a deeper level. We said earlier that you experience three things inside yourself: the world coming in, the thoughts of your mind, and the emotions of your heart. Truth is, there's a fourth thing you experience in there. It's in there all the time, but most people are so lost in the first three they don't focus on this fourth object of consciousness. Nevertheless, there is a very powerful energy flow inside of you. In different cultures it has been called by different names, such as shakti, chi, or spirit. For the purposes of our discussion, we will use the traditional yogic term *shakti*.

Once you quiet down enough, you will realize this energy is constantly flowing inside of you. You sometimes even make reference to it when your energy level suddenly changes. You say things like, "When she told me she loved me, I got so filled with energy I was floating on a cloud. I could feel it rushing through me for days." In other situations, you say, "When she told me it was over, I hardly had the energy to drive home. It left me so drained I couldn't go to work for a week." These statements are referring to the surface level of the energy we're discussing. There is a much deeper, core flow that you will experience as you transcend your personal self. It is this deeper energy flow passing through the open heart that you experience as the sensation of love. Because the energy can only go as high as you let it, this beautiful love experience does not happen that often for most people. Nonetheless, there is almost always some energy flowing through your heart creating your normal emotional state.

The reason the energy flowing through the heart fluctuates so much is because of the samskaras you've stored inside. You inwardly shoved away the experiences you didn't like having and clung to the ones you did. These unfinished energy patterns are real, and they act as blockages to your inner energy flow. When your energy tries to flow up, and it is always trying to flow up, it cannot because it hits these blockages. The energy of the shakti flow is much subtler than that of the samskaras—so the shakti can go no higher.

Before we delve further into the shakti flow, let's take a look at what happens when a blockage gets hit, or activated, by a life experience. You may never have thought about it, but you know all too well what happens. When any particular blockage gets hit, the energy held in that blockage activates, and you start feeling the emotions and thinking the thoughts that are associated with the past experience. Your inner state becomes dominated by the unfinished energy patterns stored inside, and you become totally lost in them. In this state, you are not in charge of your thoughts or emotions. Nor are you in charge of the opening or closing of your heart. The activated samskara has taken over your life. If you're not careful, it will determine your future by the choices you make in that unclear state.

Here's an example of what the mind sounds like when a samskara has been hit: "I can't believe he said that. My father used to say stuff like that to me, and I hated it. That's why I left home so young. No way I'm going through that again. I don't need to be in a relationship with someone who reminds me of my father." As logical as that may sound—it's not. This person you are interacting with is not your father, and if you didn't have those samskaras left from your relationship with your father, you would probably be handling your current relationship much better. In the truest sense, what was said didn't bother you—it hit the samskara, and the activated samskara bothered you. Regardless, to protect yourself from the disturbance, you closed your heart. *Your samskaras are what cause your heart to open and close.*

CHAPTER 23

Dance of the Energy Flow

There is a very important interaction between the energy flow and your blockages. The energy is trying to come up, but it can't because you stored these unfinished patterns from the past. It is these past impressions that determine your preferences in life. If someone manages to stimulate a negative past impression, you will not like them. If they manage to stimulate a positive past impression, it may be love at first sight. It is very dangerous to live this way—you are not in charge of your life, your past impressions are.

If you work on yourself, there will come a time when you fully understand your heart. When you have let go of enough blocked energy patterns, you will begin to experience so much energy flowing inside that you will understand firsthand what the Bible means by "...out of his heart will flow rivers of living water" (John 7:38 NKJV). There will be a constant upward flow of energy coursing through your entire system. When you get really open, it will flow out various energy centers like your heart, the point between your eyebrows, and the palms of your hands. You will become a being of light, a being of energy. That is when the energy is free to flow—when it is not obstructed by these personal blockages. We're going to discuss this in later chapters, but mentioning it now allows you to understand why your heart opens and closes in certain situations. The reason should be obvious by now—the state of your heart is dependent upon what samskaras are being activated at any given time.

Whenever you shove an obstacle into any energy flow, it will create a disturbance in the flow. It is these disturbances that you experience as emotions. Let's say you were very open and feeling a clean flow of love through your heart. Then your lover said something you took offense to, and you resisted. Your heart will no longer feel love; instead it will feel anger, fear, or jealousy. These disturbing energy patterns are the direct result of you shoving a blockage into your heart's energy flow. All these emotions are the same energy manifesting differently depending upon the nature of the blockage being hit. It is interesting that we choose to give names to these disturbances. Just look at all the names we give to our different emotions.

So far we've discussed the energy flow hitting just one blockage at a time. The more blockages there are, the more complicated the disturbances will become. Eventually, the disturbances will start to hit each other and create very complex patterns of energy. This is what it's like to live inside ourselves. This is why emotions are so powerful and often complex. You can have a love/hate relationship with something because you have patterns inside that can generate different energy flows at different times. Whatever samskara is most activated at any given time will determine what is affecting your energy flow the most. We are very complex creatures to predict, and this is why.

Unfortunately, things can get even worse. At some point, enough samskaras can be shoved into the heart so that you become totally blocked, tired, and completely uninspired. Your naturally uplifting energy flow stops supporting you. This is the power of these samskaras. They totally run our lives.

Remember that your energy is always trying to flow. The only reason it can't is because it's blocked. Like in a dammed-up river, the flow tries to find a way around the blockages. To the extent that some energy can navigate around a blockage, you will feel some strength. But that energy flow is conditioned by its ability to continue flowing that way. If something happens that stimulates yet another stored blockage, the energy flow will be affected accordingly. This is why people have so many moods and why they cannot be trusted to remain steady in their behavior. By the time the energy flow manages to find a narrow pathway around all that stuff we have stored inside, we become very narrow-minded about how the world needs to be to support that flow. Our entire personality, with its very particular likes and dislikes, is simply the expression of the pathway the energy managed to find. Our ability to feel love, joy, and inspiration is determined by how much energy makes it through the blockages.

Now you understand why your heart is so sensitive. Depending upon how well the energy can navigate around the stored blockages, your heart will open or close. Pay attention to this. Otherwise, you're going to let the opening and closing of your heart run your life. If you're talking to someone and they start discussing a subject that you have blockages about, your heart may start to close. If your reaction is to walk away and avoid that person in the future, the blockages are running your life. Similarly, if someone starts talking to you about a subject that opens you up, all of a sudden they're your best buddy and you want to hang out with them more.

Letting this opening and closing of your heart run your life is certainly not spiritual. You're not being true to yourself—you're being true to your blockages. That's all your psyche is. *Your psyche is the net result of all your blockages and how the energy manages to flow through them.* As the fluctuations in the energy flow cause your heart to change, your thoughts will change. It's actually very sad because you will end up lost in there. Those stored blockages will dominate your life, and that is no way to live. You won't go anywhere meaningful; you'll just go around in circles. There is no actual purpose, intent, or direction to such a life—except to minimize the suffering and get a periodic rush. These samskaras are from the past. They are things that happened to you in your past that you were not able to handle. Now they are determining your present, and they will determine your future if you are not careful.

We could not be discussing anything more important. These stored patterns are going to determine where you go, what inspires you, who you marry, and whether you get divorced. You're not determining your path through life—they are. Until you get very centered in witness consciousness, you are going to follow your thoughts and emotions, and they are determined by your samskaras. Surely you've been there. All that has to happen is for the energy patterns flowing through the heart to shift, and everything changes. Next thing you know, you're leaving your spouse or your job. These stored patterns represent the lowest part of your being. They are the result of you not being mature enough, or evolved enough, to handle the passing events in your life. These patterns became stuck in you and are now determining your energy flow and your entire perception of life.

Understanding the effects of these blockages helps explain why it's so difficult to make personal decisions. What you're trying to see is how one choice or the other will make you feel. "Should I marry this person, or should I wait until I establish my career?" You're using these thoughts to see how the different choices will shift the flow of your energy through your blockages. The problem is you have so many conflicting blockages stored in there that what to do is not clear. Of course it's not clear; you're consulting your inner mess and expecting a clear response. All the while, you are noticing that these thoughts and emotions keep shifting inside. The important question is not what to do about this, it is: Who is noticing all this? The same consciousness is aware of this entire process going on inside. There may be many samskaras in there, but there are not many of you in there. There is only one consciousness watching all these competing patterns and identifying with them.

When you become one integrated seer—the single witness watching all these different things pass by inside—you are centered. You are clear. You are free. But when you don't sit in the seat of the witness, and your sense of being is split amongst all these diverse inner patterns, things become very confusing. It's almost as though each path the energy takes through your field of samskaras creates a slightly different personality. You're one person around this friend and you're another person around someone else. You can even have totally different inner dialogs going on when you're around different people. Look at what happens when you go to your childhood home or a high school reunion. The surroundings stimulate past samskaras, and you begin to think and feel the way you used to in that environment. Amazingly, in these situations you feel completely at home with these different versions of yourself.

People in this state struggle to find themselves. They feel they must choose which of these personalities is really them. The answer is quite clear: none of them are you. Please don't pick one of them and let that choice determine your life. None of your thoughts are more you than any other thought. You are the one who is experiencing the thoughts. There's not a single thing about those shifting energy patterns that is you.

It is certainly difficult knowing what to do when all that inner commotion going on. The only lasting solution is to realize that it's the same you noticing all of it. You are the one who is aware that your thoughts and emotions are shifting. It happens to us all the time. Just relax and be the one who notices. Be the One who sees the many—this is the path to self-realization.

CHAPTER 24

The Cause of Moods and Emotions

Emotions are generated when your core energy flow hits a blockage. To understand this, imagine walking up to a stream that's flowing with no impediments. There are no rocks or other obstacles in the streambed. Under these conditions, the water in the stream is going to flow in a very even, undisturbed manner. There will be no eddies, sprays, or intersecting currents. This clear stream is analogous to your core energy flow, the shakti. Both of these flows are perfectly pure and constantly flowing when in their natural state. What if we put a rock into the pure flow of the stream? All of a sudden there are noticeable disturbances. There are eddies, split currents, and a spray where the flow hits the rock. Just that one rock caused a disturbance in the force. The same thing happens if we put blockages in the flow of shakti. These blockages—these samskaras—create obstacles to the shakti flow, and as such, create disturbances in the flow. These inner ripples, sprays, and eddies, combined with the release of the disturbed energy stored within the samskara, are what we call emotions. *An emotion is caused by the shakti hitting the blockages in your heart and shooting out to release the blocked energies.* This creates enough disturbance to your normal flow that your attention gets drawn to these disturbed energies. Emotions are a release of blocked energy. This goes for both negative and positive emotions.

Remember that samskaras got stored in there for a reason—you couldn't handle the experience that happened. These blockages may have been in there for years, even decades, and when something hits them, they become activated and start to release their pent-up energy. By definition, the resultant emotions and thoughts will be very personal to you. After all, you're the one who held the blockage inside to begin with. You walk into a kitchen, smell a smell, and your entire state changes because it smells like what your mother used to cook. Just a smell, and suddenly a powerful change will come over you. Your heart will get softer or harder, depending on how you interacted with your mother. Most of the time, you have no idea what is happening. You just buy into the shift of your emotions and behave accordingly.

You can now understand where your moods come from. When you reach a state of clarity, there are no moods. There is just the beauty of the clean energy flow feeding you day and night. In later chapters we're going to discuss what it's like to get clean, to get clear, to live in a state where you are always high. Until you reach that state, it's just one mood after another as the energy shifts due to these stored patterns.

From a yogic point of view, here's what happens on a daily basis in our lives. The energy flow comes up, and as it approaches the heart it can do one of three things. First, if the energy is totally blocked by the samskaras while trying to go into the heart, you won't feel your heart. A lot of people don't feel their heart very much. They are so used to focusing on their mind that they don't notice the shifts in the heart until those shifts are too strong to ignore. Emotions are messy and much too sensitive, so people suppress them. They want to be analytical, not emotional. No one told these people that if they bothered to do the work necessary to clean out the heart, the increased energy flow coming into the mind would result in more inspiration, more creativity, and more intuitive brilliance.

A second thing can happen with energy coming into the heart. It can make it in and begin hitting the blockages stored there. This tends to make you moody and more sensitive to what is going on around you.

Every once in a while, however, things will line up just right, and your heart will get quiet. Somebody is in front of you and somehow the way they look, the way they talk, or something else about them stimulates and rearranges your samskaras just right. "Her hair looks like my sister's hair, and I really got along with my sister. Look at those glasses. They're just like the ones my favorite actress wore in my favorite movie of all time. This is definitely my kind of person." The next thing you know, you're saying out loud, "People told me nice things about you, and I was really excited to meet you. Now that I see you, it's way beyond anything I expected." So it begins—love at first sight. The words are right, the hair is right, the glasses are right. Everything is opening you. You don't have to do anything—it's all happening by itself. The stimuli coming in through your senses are rearranging the samskaras just right to create an opening for the energy to come up. As the energy comes up into the heart, it has the opportunity to flow out and connect with what caused it to open.

Now we're talking about a very personal and sensitive subject. Have you ever felt the energy start to flow out of your heart? Have you ever felt your heart connect with another person? It's as if there were an energy flow tying two hearts together. People who are in love can just sit together not even talking while that beautiful, connected flow is happening. It's almost as if nothing in this world is as beautiful as that sensation of energy pouring out through the heart and connecting with someone. From a yogic point of view, what you are experiencing is shakti pouring out of the fourth energy center, the *heart chakra,* of your energy system. Though this heart center is really beautiful, it is actually not so high, since there are seven such chakras that control your inner energy flow. The yogi understands that if all the energy goes out through the heart center it will not have the power to reach the higher centers.

What you will come to realize is that the chakras are like a T-pipe fitting.

At the bottom there is an entry point for the energy, and it could be open or blocked. If it is blocked, no energy will enter that center. If it is open, the energy will come up into the center and attempt to flow right through. Should the upper pathway be blocked, however, the energy will flow out horizontally and connect with whatever stimulated the opening experience. Now as human beings, we really like that experience of energy flowing out through the heart. In fact, we don't call it *like*, we call it *love*. That experience is human love, and don't worry, spirituality has no intention of taking this away from you. It's beautiful; just know that there is a higher expression of love.

This leads us to the third thing that can happen when the energy rises up toward the heart—it can make it all the way through. At this point in our journey, all you have to understand is if the energy makes it past the fourth center, there are energy experiences way higher than human love. This doesn't mean you don't experience connection with people and things. You actually connect at a much deeper level. People who say the human connection experience is the meaning of life have not experienced the higher centers. That's like saying food is the meaning of life or intimacy is the meaning of life. Yes, these are beautiful experiences, but they are conditional, and they can come and go. The meaning of life is much deeper than that.

There are much higher energy centers you are capable of experiencing, and the further you go into these centers, the more beautiful all of life becomes. But if you can't work with the heart center, you will never know the higher centers even exist. To begin to work with the heart, you must first be able to objectively watch as it opens and closes. What you will see is that the stored patterns from your past are getting activated by outside situations and causing the heart to open or close.

Take our example of love at first sight. If you had met the same person three days earlier when you were in a bad mood, your heart might not have opened. If you hadn't seen the movie with the actress she reminded you of, she might not have hit you just right. The bottom line is that you have blockages stored inside, and they are going to determine your level of openness in any given situation. All it takes is one word said in just the right way, and the heart will open. Likewise, all it takes is one word said in just the wrong way, and the heart will close. We all have different samskaras, and we are taking on new ones all the time. That is why what turns one person on, turns another person off. It is also why the heart behaves differently for the same person at different times. It's hard to believe that our moods, attractions, and repulsions are so dependent on our past, but it's true. In our normal state, we're not paying any attention to what's going on—we're just being tossed around by it.

CHAPTER 25

The Secrets of the Heart

We are now ready to go deeper into the secrets of the heart. From our earlier explorations, you recognize that the energy can flow out for a while and create the sensation of love. You also understand that since the opening of the heart is conditional upon the state of blockages, the energy flow itself is conditional and generally will not last. Yet it is possible to experience great love all the time. All it requires is a willingness to work on yourself to remove the reason your heart tends to close. For example, imagine somebody dies who means a great deal to you. Your spouse can't go to the funeral with you because of some important work. You may deeply resent that. In fact, if you're not careful, you may resent that for the rest of your life. You're playing with fire when you play with these blockages. You may lay the groundwork that will eventually diminish or even destroy your relationship with your significant other. This is not a game—storing samskaras is serious business, and it has serious consequences. If you want love to last, learn to handle these situations better. This is a secret of the heart that is best to remember.

Another very important thing to understand about the outward flow of energy through the heart is that it literally makes a connection with the other person. This connection is real, and you become attached as the energy is exchanged between you. This is not a physical attachment to one another; this is a reliance on the energy flowing between your hearts that is feeding you both energetically.

Let's look at this in detail. Your heart was closed because stored patterns from your past were blocking the energy flow. Someone shows up whose qualities and characteristics hit you just right so the energy finds a path around one of your major blockages. The blockage is not gone, but a pathway has opened up allowing the energy to flow out through the heart. That energy goes out toward the other person, and the other person's energy goes out toward you. With the help of another person, you have managed to experience what you would be experiencing if the original blockage was not there. Perhaps you used to think people didn't like you and that you were not very attractive. Someone shows up who always admires you and looks at you with tremendous love. It makes you feel so comfortable that you melt in their gaze. It's unbelievable. You don't feel that weirdness you used to feel all the time.

Though this is really beautiful, unfortunately the samskara that was blocking your energy flow is still there. The energy found a way around it, but only as long as the energy exchange with this person is still working. It's like putting a jumper in an electrical circuit. You bypassed the samskara, but now you are very attached to and dependent on that person. If they start to leave you, or if you even think about losing them, you will feel that original samskara again in all its glory. You will feel the underlying fear and weirdness you used to feel, and it may even be stronger than before. In other words, you've tied your energy flow to somebody else, and the state of your heart is now dependent upon their behavior. Surely you have noticed this pattern numerous times in your life. This is called human love. It is very beautiful, but fortunately, there is a much higher form of love that is unconditional and can last forever.

The greatest secret of the heart is revealed when you get rid of the samskaras instead of finding a way around them. If you get rid of the blockages that are restricting the energy from flowing into and through your heart, you will feel love all the time. It will always be brimming through you. Once you reach that state, if you simply wave your hand in front of your heart, you will feel waves of ecstatic love pour through you. That's how easy it will be to experience love. Love will become the core of your being. Now, go share it. By all means, share the beautiful love you are feeling. You will be able to do this without attachment or need because your love is not dependent upon anyone or anything else. You are whole and complete within yourself. We call that *self-effulgence*. To reach this great state, you must do the necessary work on yourself to release your samskaras instead of constantly trying to find a way around them.

You now understand much more about the inner workings of the heart. Thus far we've focused on how the energy can flow through the lower part of the heart or be blocked from doing so. We can call this lower part of the heart *the human heart* because depending upon how open it is, the energy flow can create the entire range of human emotions. Energy blocked in the lower part of the heart can be experienced as feelings of jealousy, insecurity, or pangs of yearning. Even anger is the result of a strong energy flow hitting blockages in the heart and shooting out. On the other hand, if the heart is open enough for the energy to make it to the middle of the heart chakra where it can flow out horizontally, the energy will be experienced as human love. It's all the same energy doing this—the only difference is how it's blocked.

There is another level of the heart that can be experienced when the upward energy flow is strong enough to pass through the middle of the heart without going out horizontally. The samskaras have to be thinned out enough, and the flow must be strong enough to pierce the middle section of the heart chakra. When this happens, the energy pours into the higher part of the heart and generates a permanent experience of pure love, strength, and overall well-being. Now we've moved out of the human heart and into what is truly *the spiritual heart*. When the shakti flows through that higher part of the fourth chakra, you will start to feel what has been described as the presence of God. This is what the great saints experienced. At this point you no longer experience yourself as human—you experience yourself as a being of energy. You will start to feel love as a natural force in the universe. It is no longer love for somebody; it is just the force of love feeding you from inside. Once you open your heart to that level, it will always be beautiful inside, as long as you choose to focus your awareness on the love instead of what is left of your lower self.

We now know what it means to open your heart. At every level, it means to stop closing it. Your heart's natural state is open. It's just like the water in a stream; its natural state is to flow freely. If something's blocking the stream, don't waste your time trying to make the water flow around the blockage—just remove it. The same is true of the flow of shakti through the heart—just remove the blockages and love will be your natural state.

Removing blockages is spiritual purification. That is what life is all about. As you remove your blockages, the energy will start to flow freely and love will no longer be something you need or something you look for. At this stage, love has nothing to do with another person or what job you happen to be doing. You feel love and inspiration all the time. You find that the natural state of your being is to love everything you do and everyone you see. You actually have to hold yourself back to contain your passion for life because there is such a powerful flow of energy feeding you from within. This is the state Christ was describing when he said, "Man shall not live by bread alone, but by every word that proceedeth out of the mouth of God" (Matt. 4:4). You no longer live solely off what is coming in from outside. Your energy is coming from within, effortlessly, from its source.

Your heart is one of the most beautiful things in creation. In time, if you work on yourself, you will come to appreciate what you've been given. Not only can your heart feed you with unconditional love, but it is the gateway to the higher centers.

PART VI

The
Human Predicament
and Beyond

CHAPTER 26

The Human Predicament

The most meaningful questions regarding quality of life are not about what you own, or what you do, they are about how you're doing inside. Most people can relate to a response similar to: "There are moments that are so beautiful I wouldn't trade them for anything. But there are also moments I don't want to last for another second. In general, I work hard to keep it okay in here." Such is the human predicament.

For most, that is a fair description of what it's like to live in there. So far our discussions have laid the groundwork for understanding why it is that way. Throughout our lives we've stored patterns inside ourselves, samskaras, based upon past experiences we resisted. We then used these stored patterns to build a self-concept consisting of what we like and don't like and how to get events in the world to unfold accordingly. If we succeed in our efforts, it's generally nice inside; if we don't, it's not.

It is important to understand that every external event is the expression of all the energies that have come together to create that event. When this flow of the event's energy comes into you, it must make its way through your mind and heart, and then ultimately merge into your consciousness. When you use your will to block an experience from passing through, the flow of energy has to find a way to keep moving. Energy can't stand still. Energy is power, and when it hits the resistance of your will it is forced to circle around itself. That's the only way energy can stay in one place. The circle is such a powerful form in creation. It allows something to keep moving yet stay stationary. This is how samskaras are formed. These stored patterns from the past keep trying to release, but you keep pushing them back down, either consciously or subconsciously.

By now, you can see how these samskaras are running your life. To begin with, they keep coming up by themselves, and that alone causes suffering. To avoid this, you have to commit a major part of your life to creating situations that make it comfortable to live inside yourself. You end up relying on your brilliant analytical mind to figure out how to be okay. Your mind does this by imagining what would work for you. It just starts making up things, playing make-believe. As these imagined thoughts arise, you can feel how they affect your blockages. You're trying to see how the world needs to be to fit you the best. "What if this person was a certain way?" "What if that person hadn't said what they said to me?" "What if I change jobs to become the boss so people would have to listen to me instead of me listening to them?" Everything going on in your personal mind is because you're either trying to match the stored patterns that will make you feel better or avoid the patterns that will make you feel worse. Both ways, the stored patterns are running your life. Don't feel bad about it; it's that way for pretty much everyone and always has been.

You now have a deeper understanding of what we'll call the predicament: *you're in there, you're not okay in there, and you have developed concepts of how everything needs to be for you to be okay in there.* If you are not careful, you will struggle to satisfy these needs for the rest of your life. A perfect example of this burden is the all-too-common practice of worrying. Why do you worry? There are only two reasons for worrying: you either worry that you're not going to get what you want, or you worry that you're going to get what you don't want. This drives you to work outside in the world to satisfy your needs. But the root of discomfort is your stored patterns from the past. You are deciding you need to do things outside in order to appease these patterns that are inside. This does not get rid of the stored patterns—it actually reinforces your commitment to them. Over time, they will continue to bother you.

Let's say you feel lonely because you don't have someone special in your life. This sounds perfectly normal, but the truth is having someone special in your life is your attempt to solve your loneliness. It does not address the cause of it. It's just like if you eat poorly and have a stomachache; you may start looking for the Pepto Bismol. If someone then asks you why you have a stomachache, please don't say it's because you can't find the Pepto Bismol. Finding the Pepto Bismol is an attempt to compensate for your stomachache—it is not related to the cause of it. The Pepto Bismol may make you feel better temporarily, but unless you change your eating habits, the stomachache will return. You will find this is true for many things you do to compensate for your discomforts.

Eventually, we wake up and realize that compensating for what's wrong is not good enough—we must solve the root cause of why we are not okay. There is a state within you that is always filled with love and a sense of happiness. Yogananda called it *ever-new joy*. It's not a joy you get tired of; it's a constantly upward-flowing, new experience of beauty. This is the solution to every problem you're having inside—make it beautiful in there. Instead of thinking that the new job will do it, the new relationship will do it, or more money and popularity will do it, do the necessary inner work to make it beautiful inside. Notice that your problems all start with, "I'm not okay in here." If you were okay, you wouldn't be worrying and complaining. You'd be in there enjoying the beauty of the experience you're having.

Enjoying your inner state doesn't mean nothing will happen outside. Nobody is saying you don't interact with the world. You just don't interact with the world in an attempt to solve your inner problems. The outside cannot solve your inner blockages. All the outside world can do is temporarily allow the energy to go around a blockage or not hit it as much. This creates some relief, but it's not going to get rid of the blockage.

Working on releasing inner blockages, instead of struggling with life to get what you want, can seem like something is being taken away from you. But if what is being taken away from you is causing suffering, this should not be a problem. If you're eating something that makes you sick, and someone wants to give you food that makes you healthy, you must first stop eating what makes you sick. This is not an act of renunciation; it's simple wisdom. Taking on this inner work does not mean you don't get married, have a job, or fully put your heart into whatever you're doing. You can do all of that, but not for the purpose of solving your inner problems. *If you are letting the avoidance of your inner problems define what you're doing, all you're doing is expressing your inner problems outside.* Say a psychologist held up a Rorschach inkblot and you got upset about what you saw in it. Is the solution to tell them to stop holding up that piece of paper? That would be ridiculous. You would not solve anything. Yet trying to solve inner problems by rearranging the outside is exactly what everybody is doing.

CHAPTER 27

The Paradigm Shift

Everyone wants to improve their experience of life. People are always looking for more joy, love, inspiration, and meaning—the question is how to achieve this. Let's do an experiment. Imagine an all-powerful force has asked you to write down some things that need to happen for you to totally enjoy your life. If you're like most people, you will write down things like a new house, a special relationship, a higher paying job, and perhaps a yearlong vacation to your favorite spots around the world. When you're done, you will be so excited to turn in that list and get your wishes granted. Unfortunately, you'll have to wait a moment because we're going to go deeper with this experiment.

If you examine your list more closely, you will see that it's not what you really want. Let's say you wrote down that you want to get married to the person you love, and you want a wedding in Maui with birds-of-paradise surrounding the ceremony. After the wedding, you want to live in a beautiful, mortgage-free house overlooking the ocean with two fancy cars in the driveway. It's the dream you've had since childhood. The problem is that's not what you really want. Your mind has played a trick on you. Say you have the wedding, the house, and the cars, just like you wanted them, but your new spouse turns out to be a real jerk. You are treated terribly, and it's obvious right from the start that this is going to be the worst marriage in human history. On top of that, you're Catholic, so you can't get divorced. Do you still want that wedding? Unlikely. So, it wasn't really the marriage you wanted. You wanted the beautiful experience that you thought the marriage was going to give you. So why didn't you ask for that?

The same thing holds true for the new job, the million dollars in the bank, and the respect of other people. Fine, you can have it all. But what if it creates so much stress and worry that you're miserable? You'd wish you could have your old job back. You didn't really want the job, the money, or the acceptance—you wanted what you thought they would give you. You wanted happiness, joy, and a sense of total well-being. How about a constant inner state of love, beauty, and inspiration at the highest level you've ever experienced? Why didn't you ask for that?

What you did was allow your strongest past experiences to define what you think will make you feel happy. It doesn't work that way. There are plenty of people who have what you wrote down on your list, and they're not always happy. There's nothing you ever experienced that left you totally fulfilled for any length of time. You have always needed more. Your entire life you've been saying, "If I get this thing I want, I'll be okay, and if I don't have to get what I don't want, I'll be fine." For your whole life, there's been a list. When will you realize that doesn't work? If you've been doing something every minute of your entire life, and you're still doing it, obviously it doesn't work. Why not go directly to the root and say, "What I want is to feel love and joy. What I want is every moment of every day to feel complete well-being as high as I've ever felt before, and to be inspired by everything I do." Now there's a list. Let's turn that one in.

The interesting result of our experiment is that it has led us away from worldliness and into the essence of spirituality. Not that worldliness is a negative term—it just means you think the answer is in the world. You think the answer lies in what's unfolding in front of you. It isn't wrong to go to the world for what you think you want—it simply doesn't work. You're trying to find something outside that matches your "samskara of the day." Once you get what you want, or avoid what you don't want, that will no longer be your major desire or greatest fear. Once that one's out of the way, there will always be the next issue coming to the surface.

Eventually, you wake up. You realize that you want to feel love. Not that you want to love someone or have someone love you—you just want to feel love all the time. If your love is not dependent on anything or anyone, it can last forever. We call that *unconditional love*. The great yoga master, Meher Baba, taught that love must spring spontaneously from within. It cannot be coerced, and it cannot be dependent upon anything. That's what pure love is. Otherwise, you have a temporary situation that just happens to match your stored patterns. Unfortunately, this will not last. You've got lots of samskaras in there. In addition, if you're in a relationship, the other person has lots of patterns of their own, quite different from yours. This is why relationships are so complicated. Not only are each person's past samskaras different, but both people have different experiences every day to add to the collection. If somebody yelled at your partner at work, they're different when they come home than if somebody was nice to them. You, of course, had your daily experiences. If your feeling of love is dependent upon your partner behaving a certain way when they come home, you're in trouble and so are they. You have enough difficulty dealing with your own samskaras; now you have to deal with theirs also.

Don't get scared. This doesn't mean you don't have meaningful relationships. There are beautiful relationships, and they can last forever. In fact, they can get more and more beautiful all the time. But they are not samskara relationships—they are not based on the world outside matching your inner patterns. They are based on unconditional love. Once love is always flowing freely inside of you, you will be pleased to share it with another person. Such love is not based on needs or expectations—it's based on pure love wishing to express itself, unconditionally.

How do you reach such a state of unconditional love and well-being? Instead of trying to get the world to match your blockages, you work on letting go of the blockages. That's the secret of real spiritual growth. That is the real paradigm shift. If you don't have the samskaras, nothing will be blocking your inner energy flow. You will feel love, joy, and inspiration all the time. If you are willing to experience the moment unfolding in front of you, you will have the opportunity to be inspired by everything. The simple fact that things exist will be sufficient to move you.

You only have two choices: *either you devote your life to getting the world to match your samskaras, or you devote your life to letting go of your samskaras.* If you choose the latter, you don't end up with both a worldly life and a spiritual life—you end up with one life. Work, meditation retreats, taking out the garbage, sweeping the floor, driving, showering, they're all the same. The same thing is going on in all your activities—you are letting go of your blockages. It's equally beneficial to be letting go of your blockages at work, when you're driving the kids to soccer, picking up the groceries, or doing whatever you're doing. Every single moment of your life, you are either naturally enjoying what is or letting go of what's keeping you from enjoying what is. If you let go of the wants and fears that are limiting you, you'll always be okay. Letting go of yourself, instead of serving yourself, is the real paradigm shift.

CHAPTER 28

Working with the Heart

We interact with life every waking moment of our time on Earth. If we are committed to growing spiritually, we must learn to use that interaction to clear out our blockages. This inevitably returns us to the heart since we store blockages there. As we've discussed, your heart experiences myriad different emotions and feelings based on the samskaras you have accumulated. Your inability to handle the breadth of these emotions keeps you locked in the human predicament of controlling life in order to be okay. If you wish to break free and live unconditionally, you must learn to clear out your heart.

The purification of your heart begins with being grateful that you have one. Your heart is like an orchestra. Have you ever watched a movie without the score? It's dead. It doesn't have any juice to it. When something happens in your life, the orchestra of your heart begins to play. It adds richness to your life by playing high notes and low notes that are generally appropriate to the events unfolding before you. Your heart is not an obstacle or a punishment. Your heart is a beautiful gift. Would you rather not have one and live your life without feelings?

Just as the human mind is something extraordinary that can take you beyond the limit of your senses, so the human heart is even more extraordinary. It can play notes from one end of the spectrum to another. Your heart can go from absolute ecstasy to deep pain and sorrow in a matter of seconds. It can raise you to heights where you feel like angel wings are carrying you to heaven, and it can bring you down to your darkest hour. Your heart is capable of doing all of that, without any effort of your own. What an amazing instrument you carry inside of you. The trouble is you're not okay with the full range of your heart. You want to control your heart so it only plays the notes you can handle.

Spirituality is about learning to thank your heart for the beautiful expressions it is creating within you. Unfortunately, you're going to find out that you can't do that all the time. There are vibrations your heart is capable of making that you're not willing to experience. It's as though you are not evolved enough to handle the fullness of your heart, so you resist it. Just like you resist the world when it is not how you want, you resist your heart when you're not comfortable with its expressions.

As you expand and grow spiritually, your range of comfort with the outside world will become wider and wider, allowing you to handle more of the moments passing before you. The same is true with your heart. As you grow spiritually, through honoring your day-to-day experiences, you will learn to become more comfortable with your heart. As a child, the first time you experienced fear or jealousy you might have been overwhelmed and had difficulty holding yourself together. Over time, you became more accustomed to these emotions and at least tried to deal with them. Perhaps the best you could do at first was control your emotions and put on the outward appearance of being okay. Though that's not necessarily so healthy, it is better than losing yourself completely and letting emotions overcome you. If you let an unbridled emotion act out externally, it has the power to change the course of your life—not usually for the better.

Little by little, as you learn to accept that emotions are a reality of life, they will come and go if you let them. This is spiritual evolution. Just as our bodies have evolved through eons of challenging outer experiences, so our souls evolve through the fires of inner experiences. It is not that a great being does not have emotions; it is that they are at peace with their emotions. They can handle the various changes their heart goes through. If somebody you know dies, it's natural to feel a sense of loss. You're going to feel a certain amount of sadness if you cared about the person. That is your heart expressing itself in harmony with what's happening. Like an instrument playing something beautiful, your heart is composing a song of sadness for you. The trouble is you're not okay with that. Eventually you will realize that the emotion itself is not the problem—the problem is you're not able to handle the emotion. We come back to the same place again and again: Do you want to devote your life to controlling the world so your heart never feels emotions you can't handle? Or do you want to devote yourself to the evolutionary work of becoming comfortable with your heart?

Just as we found with the mind, if you want to work with your heart, understand why it is the way it is. You may have noticed it can be sensitive, volatile, and difficult to live with. The heart is this way because you didn't handle the natural emotions it created, you resisted them, which stored their energy inside you. Now you're in trouble. It's bad enough that you pushed away thought patterns, but you've also pushed away the vibrations of your heart. These blocked energy patterns are making a complete mess of your heart. The heart has become out of balance, and it has stopped opening when it needs to express healthy emotions. Let's say someone does something that makes you feel fear. There are times when fear is a normal, healthy reaction to outer events. But you aren't able to handle the emotion, so you suppress it to get it out of your consciousness. Later, you hear something bad happened to that person. Instead of feeling compassion, you feel relieved. Your emotions are no longer in harmony with outer situations, instead they are releasing the blocked energies from your past experiences.

Spiritual growth is about fixing the heart and returning it to a state of well-being. It should be clear by now that the problem is not outside in the world; the problem is your inability to handle your heart's full expression of the world. Learning to handle these expressions is the solution, and it is the essence of spiritual growth. Feelings of loss or fear or anger in your heart are just objects of consciousness that Self is experiencing. They cannot harm you, unless you resist them. They actually make you richer because you experienced them. *Every experience makes you a greater person if you don't resist it.*

Come to peace with the expressions of your heart. It may seem impossible to be comfortable with emotions that are uncomfortable, but the truth is you already have experience doing that. Take Shakespeare's play *Romeo and Juliet*. As a tragedy, it certainly is not fun. Let's say a Shakespeare troupe comes through town and performs *Romeo and Juliet*. They do such a good job that you cry with a level of relief you've hardly ever felt before. The performance was completely heart-wrenching. What do you do? You tell all your friends to go see it. You say, "I cried for three days afterwards. It was unbelievable. It touched my heart so deeply. I've never felt such pure sadness. I want to see it again, and you all should come with me." Well, if a tragedy even close to that happened in real life, you would not be praising the depth of emotion—you would be scarred for life. That's the difference between accepting the expression of your heart rather than resisting it.

Creation has put a full orchestra inside you, free of charge. This makes life so much more interesting and vibrant. Learn to enjoy your heart by ceasing to resist it. It's not about losing yourself in your emotions. It's about being willing to experience them in the same way you experience a beautiful sunset. You simply let the sunset come in. You're not doing anything. You are simply allowing awareness to be aware of what is in front of it. Sometimes it's a beautiful sunset, sometimes it's a sense of loss. The process is exactly the same: consciousness is experiencing an object of consciousness. You are not clinging to it or suppressing it. You are simply experiencing it.

If you cling to the object, it stays. If you suppress it, it stays. If it stays, it will distort reality. You are no longer open to life—you have a bias for or against certain things. These samskaras are powerful packets of energy. They distort your perception of life, and you constantly pay the price. When thoughts and emotions are suppressed, they rot down there. They will pop up at different times and cause serious problems in your life. This is what Freud taught, and it was also taught thousands of years earlier in the Upanishads. Learning to make peace with your heart is a major step toward extricating yourself from the very human predicament we all find ourselves in.

CHAPTER 29

Neither Suppression
nor Expression

Though it is true that you don't want to suppress emotions, you also don't want them running your life. There is a sacred place between suppression and expression—pure experience. In this state, you are neither suppressing the energy internally nor expressing it externally. You are simply willing to experience the energy coming from your heart and mind. The sorrow of death and the joy of birth are both coming up inside and feeding your soul. They are touching you all the way to the core of your being. You are not touching them—they are touching you. There's nothing to do about it. It is all simply a gift God is giving you. The mind is free to think; the heart is free to feel. All of this leaves you at peace, in a state of gratitude. This is the way life is meant to be.

Yet you can't handle certain thoughts and emotions. You resist them, and then you build a mental world around what you have stored in there. In this state, you can only feel gratitude if you get what you want or avoid what you don't want. Eventually you wake up and realize that you have work to do, real work. That work is not outside; it is inside. That work becomes your spiritual practice. To get what you really want—joy, love, enthusiasm, and passion for every moment of your life—you need to get these stored patterns out. The problem is that while you might see this intellectually, in a very short period of time your mind is going to fight back. This is because the inner path doesn't fit the mind's habitual patterns for how to be okay.

The only data the mind currently has is based upon its past experiences, so the mind always thinks it's right. This is part of the predicament. Please understand that your mind will always think it's right. The mind is not dumb; it knows what it experienced. But it doesn't know what it didn't experience—which is an infinitely larger body of knowledge. This is why the wise sage Lao Tzu reflected that a wise man does not argue— for what purpose? You have your mindset, and another person has their mindset. All their lifelong data says one thing, and your totally different lifelong data sees it differently. There's nothing you're going to do about that, except be humble enough to realize that at any given moment the data you are taking in is less than .00001 percent of what's going on everywhere. It's meaningless; it rounds to zero. In essence, you've had a whole bunch of zero-breadth experiences that add up to zero. The personal mind is so caught up in itself, it will never want to look at that truth.

Deep spiritual teachings embrace that truth. They ask you to look at the world in front of you and realize it took billions of years for that exact moment to manifest before you. Accept that. Honor that. Surrender to that. This begins by first accepting reality, not resisting it. It's not about doing or not doing anything—it's about surrendering your initial resistance to what is. You see what's there, and then let go of all the stuff that comes up due to your stored samskaras. Inevitably, your mind is going to start talking about likes and dislikes. Just don't listen. Why would you listen to that? It's just your personal blockages superimposed on reality.

You can now understand what you are accepting and surrendering to: reality. What else is there? Reality is truth, at least for the moment. It is what's real versus past mental impressions that are simply leftover thoughts. The way to deal with these mental impressions is to realize they are perfectly natural. Reality is going to come in, it's going to hit your blockages, and your mind is going to talk about it. Fine, be that as it may—you don't have to listen. It's that simple. If you know your mind doesn't know what it's talking about, why listen? As we've seen, the personal mind can't know anything except for the data it has collected. That data is nothing compared to the universal set of data it has missed every moment. The data the mind has in there is what we call *statistically insignificant.* That's why the mind changes its mind so often. Give it one more experience, and it will view things differently. Interesting that we keep listening to it anyway.

A wise person doesn't renounce the world; they honor the reality that's unfolding in front of them. Likewise, a wise person doesn't renounce the use of their mind; they just don't listen to the personal mind because it's lost in thoughts about itself. The personal mind is not going to solve your problems. It's doing the best it can with the limited data it has, but its efforts don't generally work out so well.

Regarding the heart, a wise person allows the heart to freely express itself inwardly but does not get lost in it. Some people say, "Follow your heart." They must not be referring to the personal heart because it's all over the place on a day-to-day basis. Fortunately, there is a higher heart to follow. Once energy flows past the middle of the fourth chakra, it enters a deeper heart that doesn't change, ever. There's a constant upward flow of beautiful energy. It brings waves of bliss so powerful you can hardly focus outwardly. It wafts over you, and you settle back into this beautiful peace that surpasses all understanding. The peace you have because you got what you wanted—that's understandable. This peace comes over you and stays for no reason, completely unconditionally—that's what your higher heart has to offer you. This is the gift of your spiritual heart.

To experience your spiritual heart, you must learn to rise above your personal heart. The personal heart is very strong and very emotional. It's not easy to pierce through the personal heart, but it is possible. First, check to see if your heart's expressions are based on current reality or the thoughts in your mind. Thoughts of what went wrong in the past, and what might go wrong in the future, create emotions that are out of tune with reality. There is no end to the mess this can create in your heart. Since the energies that build up in the heart must have a channel for release, these emotions will spill over into your external life and can create quite a disturbance.

If your emotions are in harmony with the reality unfolding before you, they are generally healthy and support the quality of your life. When both your heart and mind are in harmony with reality, energies don't release outwardly because nothing is blocking them. The power of these unblocked energies passing through the lower heart can then be utilized to rise into the higher parts of the heart. Because you are neither suppressing nor expressing, the deeper spiritual states begin to unfold. You can still contribute to what's happening outside, but your actions are not personal in nature. They are simply beautiful moment-to-moment interactions with reality that are serving the flow of life.

Reaching this state requires clearing out the samskaras that are blocking the energy flow and not putting any more in there. To do this, learn to handle your heart. This takes practice, just like you practice the piano, a sport, or anything else. We will explore this process in great depth in the following chapters. What it requires is a change in attitude: You begin to accept that things are going to happen, they're going to hit your heart, and your mind is going to create thoughts to release the built-up energies. You commit to being okay with this process. This attitude of acceptance is very different from suppressing the emotions and thoughts or letting yourself get lost in them. Just honor what the heart is doing and learn to sit back and relax behind it. Emotions can become like a breeze blowing across your face—nothing to do except experience the experience.

Appreciate the work your heart is doing to push out the samskaras you have collected over the years. Your heart will do the work—all you need to do is allow the purification to take place. At first, it's not easy to relax in the face of what you've spent your life avoiding. But it is certainly worth it because the reward is love, freedom, and constant inspiration. After all, you've already been through so much pain for so little gain.

The bottom line is that you're a beautiful being. You're a being of great love, light, and inspiration. You are made in the image of God. The god who created the whole universe exists inside of you, but you don't realize that. You're lost thinking that the world outside has to be a certain way for you to be okay. This is the human predicament, and nothing is going to meaningfully change until you learn to live from a deeper place.

To get out of this predicament, you've got some work to do, and the work is on yourself. To quote Rumi, the great thirteenth-century Persian poet, "Yesterday I was clever, so I wanted to change the world. Today I am wise, so I am changing myself."

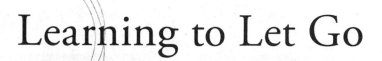

PART VII

Learning to Let Go

CHAPTER 30

Techniques for Freeing Yourself

Logically, it doesn't make sense to store inside of you the experiences that bothered you the most. If you do that, you will build your own internal house of horrors and will struggle to be comfortable inside. This is the root cause of all anxiety, tension, and psychological disturbances. This cannot be fixed until you deal with it at its root. As long as you are holding inside of you that which bothered you ten or twenty years ago, you are going to suffer.

Once your intent is to use every moment of your life to free yourself, the question becomes how to do that. Believe it or not, your sincere intent to be free is more important than any technique you can use. You're in there, and if you understand these teachings, you realize you don't want blockages in there. They make life extremely difficult. So you commit to letting them go. Traditionally, there are some powerful techniques for freeing yourself during your everyday life, and we will discuss three of them in very broad terms.

The first technique is called *positive thinking*. Yogananda used to teach that every time you have a negative thought, replace it with a positive one. This is a very basic and useful technique for bringing about change. It is based on the two types of thoughts we discussed earlier: those created willfully and those that happen automatically. If you notice your mind giving you a hard time while you're driving—those are automatically generated thoughts. You are not purposely creating them. Now try purposely creating positive thoughts about the situation. If the person in front of you is driving much slower than the speed limit, you might say inside your mind, "Wow. What an opportunity to relax. I can't be in a rush because the person in front of me won't let me. I guess it's time to watch my breath, calm down, and learn to enjoy the experience." You're welcome to do that in everyday life. You're not fighting with your mind or pushing away the negative thoughts. You're simply replacing the automatically generated thoughts with willfully created ones. Don't fight, just replace. It doesn't matter if the negative thoughts continue in the background; just focus on the positive thoughts you are willfully creating. Over time, your willfully created thoughts will replace the automatically generated ones. This is a very healthy thing to do. Simply apply your will to offset or neutralize the effect of your samskaras. Over time, this will develop a more positive mind, which is a much nicer environment to live in.

The next technique is very traditional and is broadly referred to as *mantra.* In the most general sense, "mantra" means training your mind to repeat a simple word or phrase over and over until it gets stuck in your mind. Just like a song can get stuck in your mind, a mantra can get stuck in your mind. We all experience that our minds can work in layers. You can be paying attention to someone speaking, and there can still be thoughts going on "in the back of your mind." Your mind is so brilliant it can multitask. It can create thoughts at multiple levels, and you can be aware of these layers simultaneously. Mantra is offering you a layer of mind that is always there—balanced, pleasant, a safe place to rest. As the mantra effortlessly goes on in the background, it gives you the choice of which layer of mind you want to focus on. When the habitual thoughts come up from your samskaras, you don't have to fight with them or even replace them. You just shift your consciousness onto the mantra. With positive thinking, you are continually using your will to neutralize negative thoughts with positive ones. With mantra, you are simply using your will to shift the focus of your consciousness from the samskara-generated thoughts to the mantra.

Mantra is a gift. It's like a built-in vacation. If you do the work necessary to instill the mantra in a layer of your mind, it will change your life. First off, the mantra does not have to be a traditional Sanskrit mantra like *Om Namah Shivaya* or *Om Mani Padme Hum.* It can be a name or word for God, like Jesus, Adonai, or Allah. In fact, a very powerful mantra is simply *God, God, God.* If all these seem too religious for you, a great thing to have going in your mind is: *I'm always fine, I'm always fine, I'm always fine.* How nice would it be to be reminded of any of these throughout your day?

It is not difficult to instill the mantra in your mind—all it takes is repetition. You can start practicing mantra during the time you put aside each morning and evening for your spiritual practices. Even just fifteen minutes will go a long way. A good technique is to tie the mantra to your breath going in and out. Then during the day, come back to it whenever certain events occur. For example, you could say a few repetitions of the mantra before you pick up the phone and after you put it down. It just takes a moment, and you are making a major investment in becoming a more conscious, centered being. Do it whenever you get into or out of your car, as well as when you enter or leave your house or office. No one will even notice. It is just a moment's pause that will change everything over time. Before you eat, say the mantra. If you are eating by yourself, you can have fun inwardly repeating the mantra while you chew your food. Make it a game—how many recurring events in your everyday life can you set up to remind you to practice the mantra? Here's a good use of your smartphone: set up a repeating reminder to do the mantra. Over time, you will train your mind to always have the mantra going on in the background during your daily life.

Even if you have done this work on yourself, a fateful day will inevitably arrive. Something will happen and your emotions or thoughts will start to get upset. You'll be on the verge of losing it, but the mantra will catch your attention just enough to give you the choice—go down or go up. You immediately shift your awareness off the mess and onto the mantra, and your life changes. The mantra does not stop you from having constructive thoughts; it just sits there as a safety net to catch you if you start to fall. When you have some time to actually rest back into the mantra, you will become filled with peace and well-being. It's like a vacation from the personal mind. How would you like it if the moment you sat down, tension and stress melted away as you fell back into the lap of the mantra? All this is available to you—free of charge. Just be willing to make the investment in yourself. Notice that with mantra you are learning to surrender the hold that the personal mind has on you.

The final technique we will discuss for freeing yourself from yourself is generally termed *witness consciousness,* and it includes the powerful practice of relaxing and releasing. Witness consciousness is deeper than the other techniques because, in the end, it doesn't require working with the mind. Positive thinking involves creating positive thoughts to replace the negative ones. Mantra involves creating a layer of mind that provides a peaceful and steady environment for rising above the lower layers. Witness consciousness is simply noticing that you are noticing what the mind is doing. You don't need to interact with the mind. You don't need to do anything. Just be the one who notices that the mind is creating thoughts, and you are aware of them. In order to do that, you can't be disturbed by the thoughts that are being created. If the thoughts bother you, you will leave the seat of objective observation and try to change the mind. To truly achieve witness consciousness, you must be willing to let the thoughts be as they may and simply be aware that you are aware of them.

If you want to experience true witness consciousness, just look in front of you. Do you see what's there? Don't think about it, just see it. That's witness consciousness. It's *just seeing.* You are simply witnessing what's there. Now, turn your head and look around. Practice the immediacy of just seeing. Notice that your thoughts often have something to say about what you see. Can you simply notice these thoughts like you noticed what was outside, or do you have to do something about them? Thoughts, emotions—they come up by themselves. Good, now simply notice them.

When you reach the state where you can observe what is going on in the mind and heart, you'll notice that you're not always comfortable with what's happening inside. What is more, there is the tendency to want to willfully do something about it. That's very natural. If you want to willfully do something, here's what you do—relax. This is certainly not the intuitive thing to do. You want to protect yourself from the inner disturbance by getting rid of it. That struggle just makes it worse. You are capable of simply relaxing and not engaging with the disturbed energies. At first this seems impossible because you're trying to get the disturbance itself to relax. Don't do that; *You* relax. You who notices the disturbance are not the disturbance. You are witnessing the disturbance, and you are welcome to relax in the face of it.

You are in the seat of awareness, way back inside, watching the dance of mind and heart. It's a very natural place, this place back inside. If you don't get pulled into the thoughts and emotions, you can just relax and notice. Don't think about it. The moment you see what's going on— just relax. Relax your shoulders, relax your tummy, relax your buttocks, and most importantly, relax your heart. Even if the heart itself won't relax, the area around your heart will. You have willpower in there, use it. Here's what you do with your will: relax and release. First relax through your initial resistance, then release the disturbed energy that comes up. When you do this, you are actually providing space for the release of the samskaras causing the disturbance. You are giving them more room to release because you're not struggling with the thoughts and emotions they are creating. Eventually there is no struggle, as you have created distance between the seat of Self and the noisy mind. To be free, you need distance between those two—subject and object.

Spirituality is not about changing the objects you're looking at. Spirituality is about accepting the objects but not getting sucked into them. It's about being detached and feeling at peace with whatever your mind and heart are doing. When you are totally comfortable with everything that can come from your mind and heart, they will stop creating inner disturbance. You don't know that yet, but it's true. People often ask whether the mind will keep talking once you are at peace with it. The mind is talking because you're not okay, and it's trying to figure out how to be okay by getting things the way you want. Once you're okay in there, there's much less to talk about. When you're in the presence of someone you love, you're not thinking about how to find love. You're just experiencing the beauty of the love. Likewise, when you are okay in there, you will not be thinking about how to be okay. You will just be relaxing into the quiet state of peaceful well-being. This requires that you be okay with your thoughts and emotions. Relaxing in their presence is a good start to being okay with them. If you can't willfully relax in the face of thoughts and emotions, you will have to do something about them. You will get pulled down into them and attempt to do something to fix what is bothering you. Better to simply relax and allow the samskaras the room they need to release. When you relax back into witness consciousness, you are surrendering to the reality of what's happening.

First relax, then lean away. You who notices are at a distance from what you are noticing. You don't have to think about it. Just notice that what you are seeing in there, thoughts and emotions, are all distinct and at a distance from you. Now, lean away from their noise. The mind and emotions make noise. That is not a problem. Just relax and lean away from the noise. When you lean away from the noise, you are creating distance between *You* (the consciousness) and the objects of consciousness (the thoughts and emotions). In that distance, the samskaras have room to release their energy. It's going to get uncomfortable, and that's natural. The discomfort you are experiencing is the discomfort of samskaras being released. They were stored with pain; they are going to release with pain—if you let them. This is the pain that ends all pain.

CHAPTER 31

Low-Hanging Fruit

The best way to let go of stored pockets of pain is to practice. Just as you practice scales to learn the piano or practice a sport to get good at it, so you practice letting go to learn how to do it. You start with simple things. We call these the *low-hanging fruit*. There are many situations each day when you create inner disturbance for absolutely no good reason. Bothering yourself about the car in front of you does no good at all. It only makes you tense and uptight. The cost-benefit analysis is one-hundred-percent cost and zero benefit. Letting go of that tendency should be easy, but it's not. You will find that you're in the habit of insisting and demanding that things should be the way you want, even if it's irrational. Things are the way they are because of all the influences that made them that way. You are not going to change the weather by complaining about it. If you are wise, you will start to change your reactions to reality instead of fighting with reality. By doing so, you will change your relationship with yourself and with everything else.

Start with the small things to prove to yourself that you are capable of doing this. Working with yourself at this level is practicing letting go. Once you are able to relax and release through the relatively easy stuff, you will find you are better able to deal with the bigger situations. You are training yourself to deal with yourself.

Lots of different experiences in life fall into the low-hanging fruit category. A good practice for letting go can be found in your relationship with the weather. Believe it or not, you can use the weather for tremendous spiritual growth. There's always weather out there: hot, cold, windy, dry, humid, and everything in between. The weather has nothing to do with you. It has to do with the forces that are causing it to be the way it is. If you can't handle the weather without getting disturbed, how are you going to handle anything else? Complaining about the weather is a perfect example of something that has a one-hundred-percent cost and zero benefit. What do you gain by complaining about the weather? Nothing, except to get upset. "I couldn't handle the heat today. It was terrible. I was sweating. I hated it." Congratulations, you didn't have a nice day, and it didn't change the weather one bit.

Eventually, you start to work with yourself. When your mind complains about the weather, don't fight with it. If you want, you can use positive thinking. For example, when the mind starts up with, "It's hot; I'm so hot," instead of getting into that, ask yourself, "How did it get hot? What does that mean 'it's hot'?" Use your mind to remind you that there's a star ninety-three million miles away that is so hot you can actually feel its heat. That's amazing. Use your higher mind to appreciate and respect reality instead of complaining about it. When you do this, you are willfully using your mind for something positive and constructive. You are raising yourself.

Though this practice of positive thinking is beneficial, ultimately, what you need to do is relax and release past the disturbance. If you bother to relax and release, you won't be so hot. After all, *You* in there can't get hot—you can only experience that the body is hot. You are way back inside, witnessing the experience of heat. If you relax and release back into your seat of consciousness, you are relaxing away from the part of you that's complaining. There is definitely complaining going on in the mind, no reason to deny that. But if you relax and lean away from where the noise is coming from, you will be leaning back into the seat of Self.

Two things happen when you relax and release. One, you stop fighting with the causes of your disturbed mind, and that gives them room to release. Two, you are actually relaxing back into the seat of Self, and you will grow spiritually. If you will do that with the weather, if you will do that with the car in front of you, if you will do that with all these low-hanging fruit situations, you'll grow every single day. The way to know that you are working with low-hanging fruit is that the situation is resolved simply by letting go inside. There is nothing else to do about it. You were the only problem, and once you let go of creating the problem, the problem is solved. If you accept the weather, there's nothing else to do about it. If you accept the myriad meaningless things you have decided to bother yourself about, there's nothing else to do about them. That's how you identify the low-hanging fruit.

In contrast, if you let go of your reactions to a situation and there is still something in front of you to deal with, then you have some work to do outside. If you lose your job and work with letting go of your negative reaction, that's good, but you still need to go out and look for a new job. Letting go does not absolve you of your responsibilities in life. You are not letting go of life, you are letting go of your personal reactions to life. Your personal reactions do not help you deal with situations in a constructive manner—they actually cloud your ability to make good decisions.

When all is said and done, you're going to find the majority of your inner disturbance falls into the category of low-hanging fruit. The only reason there's a problem is because you defined it that way. You are the problem, and that can't be solved outside. It can only be solved inside.

CHAPTER 32

The Past

You're driving down the street and a billboard reminds you of something that troubled you in the past. Perhaps it was an event that happened eight years ago. What is the benefit of getting disturbed by that? You just ruined your day for no good reason. Just because something bothered you in the past doesn't mean it should still be bothering you. After all, it's no longer happening. You think that since you don't want to go through it again, you need to remember how bad it was. That's like saying you need a doggy bag for the food that made you sick so you can take it home, taste it each morning, and remember how sick it made you. You would never do that with bad food, so why do you do it with bad experiences?

We are now ready to pay attention to another area that is very ripe for spiritual growth, your past. You probably won't agree at first, but it also falls under one-hundred-percent cost and zero benefit. Of what possible benefit could it be to still be bothered by something that happened before that isn't happening now? It's already over. There is zero benefit to being bothered by something that is not even happening. On the other hand, there is certainly an amazing cost: your entire mental, emotional, and even physical health.

Instead, if you let experiences pass completely through you when they are actually happening, they will touch you to the core of your being and become part of you without leaving any scars. You will simply be able to learn from the experience and grow. Once you fully digest an experience, you will naturally know how to deal with it should it happen again. If you touched a hot stove when you were a child, you don't have to keep the painful experience in the forefront of your mind. You don't need to always remind yourself that stoves are hot and can hurt you. If you do that, you will have made a samskara out of the experience instead of simply learning from it. Don't worry, you will know darn well not to touch a hot stove again.

Similarly, once you have learned a sport or a musical instrument, you don't have to keep thinking about how to play—it becomes second nature. That means it has integrated into your whole being. It becomes totally natural, and you never need to think about it again as you do it. That is how all your past learning experiences should be, effortlessly there when you actually need them, never bothering you when you don't. If you process your experiences properly, they will always be there to serve you, never to haunt you.

Perhaps this exercise will help you understand what it means to fully process something instead of having to pass it through your thinking mind. Just for a moment, glance at the scene in front of you. How hard was it for you to see it? Obviously, it took no effort at all; you just instantly saw it. What if the finest artist in the world called you on the phone wanting to paint what you saw, right then. How long would it take you to describe everything to them? We're talking about every color shade, reflection of light, grain variation in the wood, every single detail. That would be a very long phone call. Yet you saw it all in a billionth of a second. That is the difference between consciousness just seeing versus the mind trying to process what is seen.

This difference holds true for all life's experiences. When you have an experience, it can simply come in and touch consciousness directly. It doesn't need the mind to judge it as desirable or undesirable and then store it accordingly. Just as you were able to see the scene in front of you in full detail without "thinking" about it, so you can integrate the fullness of your experiences into your being without having to block them in your mind. *There's nothing richer than a fully processed experience integrated into your whole being.*

How many incidences from your past would you like to truly be done with rather than having to deal with them mentally and emotionally, long after they are ancient history? In fact, to achieve deep spirituality, your unfinished past cannot be inside of you. It must be gone—not suppressed, but gone. You will see over time that when those blocked patterns are gone, all that is left is the flow of spirit. What is left is the most beautiful thing that could ever exist.

How do you let go of the past? It's very straightforward. The past blockages will come up on their own on a daily basis, and when they do— let them go. There is no game here. It's quite simple. Outside events cause stored patterns to come up. Good, let them come up. Things are going to happen in your life that hit your samskaras. If samskaras are in there, they are going to get hit. The world is perfect for each person's growth, but not for the reason you think. The world is a perfect fit for everyone's growth because everyone is looking at the world through their own blockages. It's the same as with the Rorschach inkblot test. It's not that the inkblot is perfectly tailored to bring up your issues. It's that you are looking at the inkblot through the veil of your issues and projecting your issues onto it. That's why the same inkblot works fine for diagnosing all patients, just as the same world works perfectly for everyone's growth. If you want to see what is really out there, you need to get rid of your inner issues.

Our scientists tell us there's really nothing out there—just a bunch of atoms made up of electrons, neutrons, and protons. Our quantum physicists go even further. They tell us that there's really just a quantum field of pure energy that has both wave and particle characteristics. The subatomic particles emanating from this energy field (quarks, leptons, and bosons) are what make up our entire universe. Though you couldn't care less about these particles, the structures they create come in through your senses, hit your stored blockages, and it gets uncomfortable in there. You are doing this; the subatomic particles can't be doing this. To free yourself, the moment you notice disturbance, let go. Don't wait until that initial disturbance takes over your mind. You are perfectly aware that you're beginning to get upset before you actually get upset. You feel it. You feel when something starts to bother you. If you want to grow spiritually, that's the moment when you do the work.

This is the essence of spiritual growth. If you work on yourself, you're going to create a beautiful place inside to live. This is more important than your marriage or your family. It's more important than your job or your career. You're working on yourself directly instead of indirectly. If you create a beautiful inner environment, you can have a wonderful marriage, a wonderful family life, and a wonderful job. But if you have a mess inside, you'll just be trying to use these outer situations to make yourself okay. This can work for short periods of time, but you don't want to build your house on sand. The alternative is when the stuff starts to come up, the second you feel that change, relax. Don't even wait until you know what it's about; just relax and let go. You can work with samskaras at the energetic level rather than the mental level. This is much deeper. There are blockages in there, but they don't want to be in there. They want to come up and be released. Surrender is the act of letting go instead of resisting by pushing the blockages away. You will see it's not always comfortable when these disturbances from your past come up. The events weren't comfortable when they happened—that's why you pushed them away. Now that they're trying to release, are you going to push them back down for another ten years? If you are not serious about working on yourself, that is what's going to happen.

Eventually, you will take it seriously that the purpose of your life is letting go of these stored patterns. Your blocked past is keeping you from God, and it's keeping you from having a beautiful life. The same sincere effort you put into a relationship or into earning money, you learn to put into freeing yourself of these blockages. Remember this: It's not about renunciation—it's about purification. It's about cleaning out the inside so you can have a beautiful life, both outside and in. At some point in your growth you will recognize that freeing yourself is worth the discomfort of letting go of past disturbances. Look at what athletes go through for the Olympics. For years they put themselves through hell to win a gold medal. They feel proud for a while, then what? It becomes a wall ornament. We're talking about putting out a fraction of that effort to win everything, and the fruits of your effort will keep giving over time. Imagine not having those sensitive blockages in there. Imagine being able to enjoy the world as it unfolds around you. You can begin to appreciate life and wholeheartedly participate in it. What's that worth?

This is what happens when you are willing to let go of your past. This is a very important spiritual practice. You should be able to look back on your past and say, "Thank you." It doesn't matter what happened. Remember, every moment there are trillions and trillions of things going on in the universe, but you only get to experience one. How can you not appreciate the one you got to see? You came down to Earth, and this was the experience you had. That's what your life is: the sequence of experiences you got to experience. Learn to love and appreciate your past. Fully embrace it, thank it for teaching you, and let go of any judgment that there was something wrong with it. Your past is uniquely yours. It happened. It's sacred. It's beautiful. Nobody else ever had it, and nobody else ever will. Embrace your past, hug it, kiss it—love it to death.

CHAPTER 33

Meditation

Many practices can help you on your spiritual journey. As you do them, always remember that your intent is to cease storing blockages. If weekend retreats help you with the process of letting go, then do them. If a form of therapy helps you open up and release, then do it. A time-honored technique for spiritual growth is meditation. In order to meditate, you have to let go of your traditional relationship with your mind and emotions. There are many forms of meditation, but the bottom line of all of them is letting go of your addiction to focusing on your thoughts. Focus on your breath, count, do mantra, feel the energy—in other words, focus on anything except the thoughts arising in your mind. As you practice meditation you will find that your ability to let go during daily life is greatly enhanced. Relaxing and releasing on the meditation cushion is the same process as relaxing and releasing during daily activity. Eventually, you will find that you remain clearer throughout the day— you are always aware of what is going on both inside and outside. This clarity of presence is one of the gifts of meditation.

There are many meditation techniques. If you don't have a technique, you can try this simple practice. Commit to sitting down for a short period twice a day, preferably at the same times each day. This requires the discipline to give this inner work priority over everything else. Most people manage to eat and sleep at certain times each day; they also manage to find time for their jobs and their relationships. This inner work on yourself is more important than everything else you do. In the end, it will affect the quality of your life more than all the other things you do each day. Many of today's teachers say that to sit in meditation for fifteen minutes in the morning and fifteen minutes in the evening is a good starting point. That alone will create great benefits. Just put aside the time to sit down in a quiet place.

What do you do during that time? What you don't want to do is expect to have a spiritual experience. If you expect that, you're going to get disappointed and you will stop meditating. You are sitting down for the same reason you sit down to play your scales on the piano, to learn. If you sit down to practice the piano and expect to be playing Beethoven when you get up, you're going to quit the piano. The same is true of meditation. The reason you sit down to meditate is to learn how to remain conscious inside while your mind creates thoughts and your heart creates emotions. Whatever is going on in there is fine—as long as you can objectively observe it. This is called *mindful meditation.*

Suppose someone says, "I can't meditate. I sit down, and my mind doesn't shut up. It just keeps talking and talking." That's actually a pretty good state—you know you're not your mind. You actually watched your mind talk for fifteen minutes and noticed that it didn't shut up. You don't normally notice that. You normally get all involved in the thoughts the mind is creating. This time you noticed them, and you noticed that they did not stop. That, in and of itself, is a form of witness consciousness. You were witnessing the thoughts instead of getting lost in them. Don't call that a bad meditation. If you practice the piano and make mistakes, that's not a bad practice session. Every practice session is about learning. Likewise, there is no such thing as a bad meditation—there is just practicing being aware of what is going on in there.

Of course, there are higher states of meditation than simply noticing the mind, but you should not set expectations. Expectations are just another mind-trip. Decide that you are sitting down because you choose to learn to be present and work on yourself. This is a time when you don't have so many external distractions, so you can practice being present. That's all. You may not like what you see inside, but you are learning to be present with it. You're learning to be at peace with what used to drive you crazy.

To appreciate the purpose of spiritual techniques, you have to realize that you are addicted to your mind. You're more addicted to your mind than people are to drugs. In fact, the reason many people start doing drugs is to get away from their mind's incessant chatter. That's also why some people start drinking—the mind can be impossible to live with. If you are like most people, you are addicted to every single word your mind says. If your mind suddenly says, "I don't like it here, I want to leave," you leave. If it says, "I think something good will come from being here, I want to stay for a while," you stay. You are absorbed in your thoughts, and you follow whatever the mind says. In essence, your mind is your guru, and you need to back off from that relationship.

Changing your relationship with your mind is a major part of the spiritual journey. You don't do this by fighting with the mind and resisting thoughts. You do this by learning not to listen to the mind. You are the consciousness, and the mind is the object of consciousness. You must be able to withdraw your attention from the mind, even when the mind is talking. The easiest way to do this is to pay attention to something else. One very common meditation technique is to pay attention to your breath. Just watch your breath. Over time you will see that if you are watching your breath go in and out, you are not focusing on the mind. If you try this very simple technique of watching your breath, you'll see how addicted you are to the mind. One moment you're sitting there watching your breath and not being distracted by the mind. The next thing you know, you're lost in your thoughts. That is what's going to happen. You may not be able to sit there for fifteen minutes and watch your breath. Good, that shows you how strong your addiction is to the mind.

The reason you lose focus on your breath is that consciousness gets distracted by what your mind is saying. In other words, you stopped watching your breath, and you started watching your mind. The moment you catch on that you've done that, don't get down on yourself. Just start watching your breath again. The entire purpose is to practice gaining control of your attention so that it becomes yours again. What you pay attention to determines your experiences in life. You should have the right to consciously decide what to pay attention to. Until you learn to back away from the mind, you have no choice; you pay attention to whatever your mind says.

There is one more element you can add to this simple meditation technique we've been discussing. You're not going to know right away that you stopped watching your breath. You're going to get lost in your mind, and maybe fifteen minutes will go by. To help notice sooner, instead of just watching your breath, count your breaths. Simply count a round of inhale/exhale as one, then two, and so on. But don't count to one hundred. Count to twenty-five and start over. That way you will see sooner that you drifted off the breath. In/out...one, in/out...two, in/out...three. Watch your breath go in and out of your abdomen. Just sit there and watch your breath while you count to twenty-five, and then go back to one. If you find that you're at forty-three, just start over at one. Not a thought about it, just immediately start counting at one. You now have a job to do that requires you to be present. You must be conscious enough while watching your breath to know to go back to one after you reach twenty-five. This doesn't require thought—it just requires awareness.

Some people turn mala beads during meditation, others do mantra. These are just ways to help keep your consciousness on something other than your wandering thoughts. So, meditation is easy—if you understand that it's not about having spiritual experiences. Please don't worry about that. Just practice being present. If you do this on a regular basis, you're going to find that you are consciously aware during the day when your samskaras get hit. Now it's just a question of your level of commitment. Every single time you start to get disturbed, are you willing to relax and release? Or do you still need to go through another round of expressing and defending your blockages?

CHAPTER 34

Handling the Bigger Stuff

Real spiritual practice entails devoting every moment of your life to your liberation. Life is your real guru. It's challenging you to either move further away from Self or come back to Self. Life is your friend. Everything that happens in life is an opportunity to get better at freeing yourself from yourself—dying to be reborn. If you sincerely work on releasing the low-hanging fruit, and if you remain centered in the seat of Self as your past samskaras are released, you will become a more conscious being. You will no longer have to come back to center after a difficult conversation, you will remain centered during the entire experience. At first, this is difficult. Just keep working on it. Make this the most important thing in your life—because it is. It really is the only rational way to live your life. It's not a religious technique; it's simply deciding to wake up and make something great of yourself.

If you constantly let go, you will eventually achieve a state of perpetual presence. You will be established in the seat of Self, and you will never leave that seat again for the rest of your life. No matter what happens, no matter who dies, no matter who leaves you, no matter what. All that stuff can still come up, but you will have the power to decide what to do about it. There will be time you never had before, between the event and your reaction to it. Things start to unfold as if in slow motion—even reactive thoughts and emotions. This gives you time to relax and let go.

We are now ready to address the bigger stuff. As you let go, and there is less small stuff, the bigger things will come up all by themselves. You may start having very intense dreams. You may be driving in the car and begin feeling powerful emotions for no apparent reason. Good, you don't need a reason. It is simply energy, the shakti, trying to push up because you have given her the room to do so. She is your best friend. This energy flow inside is helping you, and it's always trying to push up. You don't need to do anything except keep letting go. What if something happens that's a really bad situation? The house catches fire. You lose your job. That's certainly not low-hanging fruit. If you are sincere on this path, what do you do? First let go. Always let go of your human reaction first. If you are upset and cannot deal with the situation, what good are you? If you can't handle the sight of blood, you are of no use at the scene of an accident. First let go of your personal reaction so that you can serve the situation to the best of your ability.

Let's take a real-life example. You get a phone call informing you that your sixteen-year-old son had drugs in his school locker. Difficult things like this happen in the world. You may not like it, but you are going to have to deal with it. Perhaps your mind starts up, "How could he do this to me? Oh, my god, what did I do wrong? My husband's going to be so mad at me. We're having enough trouble in our relationship. This could be the end of my marriage. Why do I deserve this?" What on Earth has all that personal melodrama got to do with your son's problem? Those are your problems, and you need to let them go. You're not supposed to be interacting with the world outside based on your blockages inside. All that personal talk has nothing to do with the problem at hand. It has to do with the fact that this situation hit your blockages, and now you're reacting to your issues instead of your child's issue. If you allow that to happen, you're going to make every decision based on what makes you feel better, which is likely not what is best for the situation at hand.

If you take things personally, you will try to protect yourself by avoiding disturbing experiences. But difficult situations present an opportunity to change that dynamic. The way to do that is to let go of your entire personal reaction to the situation. You just let it go. You don't let go of the situation—you let go of your reaction to the situation. Go to the principal's office, but not to protect yourself. Go because your son needs help. Go because the principal needs help with the situation. Go because you're the parent, and your son is your responsibility. Do your best to raise the energy in a constructive manner. You can't do this if you're focusing on your embarrassment, fears, and other personal reactions.

Bottom line, you let go of the personal so you can interact properly with what's in front of you. It's the same thing in business. You're in a meeting, and they're discussing a project. You have a bright idea that you want to contribute. So you put it out there, but it gets shot down. That hurts. Of course it does. You have an ego in there, and it's going to get bothered. Now for the rest of the meeting, either you don't contribute anything because you're sulking, or you keep bringing up proof that what you said wasn't so dumb. You no longer belong in that meeting. Your presence has become about you, not about the project. You can't work like that. Your underlying motive can't ever be about you. It has to be about serving what's happening in front of you. To the absolute best of your ability, you always serve life as it unfolds before you.

The process of letting go becomes how you work on yourself. Your only decision is: Are you going to let go or not? It's your choice. Either you're working on yourself on a regular basis or you're not. The blockages inside you that generate personal thoughts and emotions are nothing but leftover samskaras. They are based on past issues you couldn't handle, and they will tend to lead you in the wrong direction. Learn to express your higher Self. Express the deeper part of your being that's in harmony with life.

Keep letting go. The entire spiritual path is letting go of yourself. What will happen if you do this? That's what we'll explore next. We're going to deal with what life is meant to be like for every single person. Regardless of what has ever happened to you or what you've ever done—it really doesn't matter. If you let go of the samskaras inside of you, they will no longer affect your life. You can truly be free of your past. This is what *living untethered* means. It means to let go of yourself, to transcend your personal self as Buddha taught, to die to be reborn as Christ taught. It is the essence of all spiritual teachings, and it is the truth. Everyone is capable of freeing themselves, if they are willing to do the inner work.

PART VIII

Living a Life of Acceptance

CHAPTER 35

Dealing with Blocked Energies

One thing is for certain, we are all conscious inside. The question is: What are we conscious of? Pretty much everyone is aware that there are constantly changing energies within that can be overwhelming at times. Even if they don't understand the energies, to stay upright in life, people either push the energies away or try to release them through outer expression. Though both these efforts cause their own sets of problems, they are better than drowning inside.

When people are actually drowning in water, what do they do? They try to grab something solid, like a board floating by, so they don't sink. That is how most people live their lives. They are grabbing onto whatever they can so they don't drown. Generally, what they're grabbing onto is something outside themselves. They think that if others respected them more and treated them better, it wouldn't be so caustic inside. If someone would just truly love them and be loyal to them, then they'd be okay. The problem is, if they manage to get what they want, they will grab ahold for dear life and never let go, which creates its own issues. Even worse, if the outside world ever stops giving them what they want, they will start to drown again.

If you want to see how much you cling to the outside world in order to avoid drowning inside, just see what happens when the world doesn't unfold the way you expect. What happens when someone very close to you behaves in a way that doesn't align with your model? Your mind and heart catch fire. This happens even if the person hasn't actually done anything. All that is needed is for your mind to think, "What if my husband leaves me? Sally's husband left her. If Sam ever left me, I would just die." That's all it takes, and you feel pain and disturbance. All the energies become unsettled inside. Why does this happen? It happens because you've been trying to build a place of solidity within your mind that you can hold on to. As long as everything reasonably reinforces that, you feel safe and relatively okay. But you have distanced yourself from the core of your being by clinging to something outside. That's what we do, and it doesn't work. If you want to grow spiritually, if you want to have a beautiful life instead of a midlife crisis, you need to do the inner work.

A midlife crisis happens when you've been building and clinging and fighting for half your life in order to be okay, and you're not. You're simply not free and at peace inside, even though you have the kids, the marriage, the job. As it turns out, midlife crises are perfectly reasonable. It's surprising more people don't have them. Halfway through your life, you realize it hasn't worked—you're still not okay. Sure, you're okay as long the spouse behaves, the kids do well in school, and you get respect at your job. As long as all this happens, and your finances hold up, you're conditionally okay. But inside you know it can change on a dime, so you must keep struggling to stay ahead. That's why life is a struggle.

The alternative is to clean up the mess inside. Someday you will realize you are not drowning. You're simply sitting on a planet spinning around the middle of absolutely nowhere. That's the truth of the matter. The Cassini spacecraft took a picture of the Earth from two million miles out. The Earth is just a small dot in the middle of dark, empty space. How can you drop down onto the nicest planet there is and not be okay? We've looked far and wide with our space telescopes, and we haven't found anything, anywhere, even close to the majesty of the Earth. Basically, you won the lottery! You dropped down onto this phenomenal planet that's always exciting, challenging, and growthful. It has all sorts of colors, shapes, and sounds—it's unbelievably amazing. Yet, what do you do? You suffer. Why? It's not the planet causing you to suffer—it's the stuff you have stored inside.

The logical questions become: Why are you storing all this stuff inside you? And if you're going to store stuff inside, why not make it nice stuff? People collect all sorts of things as hobbies. Some collect spoons, teacups, stamps, or coins from all over the world. But you had a brilliant idea for a hobby—let's collect bad experiences. That's what you did: "I'm going to collect every bad experience I ever had and keep it inside me so it can bother me for the rest of my life." How can that work out well? If you keep doing it, you're going to collect more and more bad experiences, and your life will get heavier and heavier.

Are you really going to continue making your life so difficult? *In essence, you are causing yourself to be unhappy, then you're going outside and demanding that the world somehow make you happy.* The world cannot make you happy while you're inside making yourself unhappy. It's that simple. You have to work on letting go of the root cause of suffering. The spiritual path is always about letting go of yourself, and that means dealing with the blocked energies.

The blocked energies inside are going to build up and need release if you don't deal with them. These energies may release in the form of anger, verbal or physical fighting, and other bursts of uncontrolled behavior. When you allow the energies to release unconsciously like this, you're not in charge. The energies will tend to follow the path of least resistance, as determined by the samskaras. When you allow this to happen, the uncontrolled energy carves channels within you that will make it easier to flow that way again. The energy flow becomes a habit. Not only is "losing it" unhealthy because of what you may say or do outside, but you also increased the probability of losing it in the same way again. This can cause all kinds of trouble. Any time you're not in charge in there, there's going to be trouble. It's that simple.

Understanding this process of blocking and then expressing energies helps us have compassion for our own past behaviors, as well as for others. Compassion means you understand the root cause of people's behavior. People have trouble handling their blocked energies, and in most cases, they have not been taught how to channel the energies to a higher level. There is a higher level of our being, and those lower energies can be raised up. You have access to a much higher way to deal with inner energies than to simply step aside and let them express. That doesn't mean they should be suppressed. Your choices are not limited to expression or suppression. As we will discuss, there's a third choice, transmutation, and that's where true spirituality comes in.

CHAPTER 36

Transmutation of the Energy

Suppression blocks inner energy; unchanneled expression wastes its power. The highest use of the energy is *transmutation*. Most people know nothing about transmuting the energy, yet it is the essence of spirituality. Currently, your natural energy flow is blocked by the samskaras in your lower energy centers. When the energy tries to release, you either push it back down or allow it to blow off some steam externally. This external release solves nothing in the long run—the energy will just build back up behind your blockages. The release is temporary because the cause of the blocked energy has not been addressed.

What if, when the energy tries to come up, you see it as an opportunity to get rid of the blockage it's hitting? The energy is going to attempt to release the samskara by pushing it out of the way. The problem is if the blockage was stored with pain, it's going to come back up with pain. Instead of pushing it back down because you can't handle the experience, or releasing it outside as a way of relief, you can relax and release at such a deep level that you allow the blockage to pass without resistance. That is what *transmutation of the energy* means. It involves using the rising energy as a positive force by allowing it to cleanse whatever was blocking it.

This is the highest way to work with your inner energy—use it to grow spiritually. Use it to let go of the blockages that are keeping you trapped. It is those blockages that cause suffering. They only allow you to be okay if things are a certain way. This creates discomfort, anxiety, and fear about life. That discomfort drives people to seek all sorts of distractions, which just creates more turmoil. We all know about this cycle of disturbance and temporary relief. Now you know there is a much higher way to live. If you are willing to release the blockages, over time the energy will find its way up. It will push the samskaras out of the way, and the next thing you know, you won't even be able to relate to how you used to be. This is especially true about how you used to deal with some people around you. You'll wish you could go back and say, "I am so sorry. I was so lost." You will see how relationships used to be about finding a way to be more comfortable with yourself. Once the blockages begin to clear, the energy will find its way into your heart, and that will comfort and sustain you. Relationships will naturally be about love and caring—all of them will be about serving others. They will no longer be about control or getting something you need. This is what happens as the energy is free to rise within you.

If you release the blockages, the energy will naturally rise higher. You will not have to fight with it—the energy wants to come up. Always remember, the energy wants to go up. You do not have to force it. It is best for long-term spiritual growth if the energy is allowed to rise naturally. When you get blockages out of the way, you will feel a steady upward flow of energy. Eventually, you will realize that the shakti wishes to express something so beautiful, it will leave you breathless. You will begin to know a peace that "passeth all understanding" (Phil. 4:7). You won't need anything. Your natural state is so beautiful; you are whole and complete within yourself. It simply depends on your willingness to work with the energies. If you do, shakti will go higher and higher until eventually it moves as fountains of joy flowing out the higher energy centers. As it does, your entire relationship with this world will transform into something very beautiful. What you were trying to get from the outside will now naturally be going on inside. You will become filled with love and ecstasy. Again, Christ described this as: "Man shall not live by bread alone, but by every word that proceedeth out of the mouth of God" (Matt. 4:4). You will have a perpetual flow of energy feeding you from within.

The transmutation of the inner energy flow is the answer to all the world's woes. If people felt whole inside and were fed by the constant flow of love and deep peace, they wouldn't be fighting with each other. Why would you kill, rob, or harm someone if you were content within yourself? It is only because people are struggling inside that they are driven to struggle outside. That's the only reason we need so many rules and laws. People left to their own create great trouble struggling with their inner disturbances. There is something much higher within us, and it happens to be our natural state. You're a beautiful being; a truly awe-inspiring being. But you can't reflect that beauty if you're not okay. No matter how beautiful you are, if you are trying not to drown, you're not going to seem so beautiful. To stop struggling once and for all, work on letting go of the blockages.

A spiritual being views life as follows: "I came down to the planet Earth for a short time, and these are the experiences I got to have. They were challenging, but I handled them and am better off because of them." You don't suppress your issues, and you don't allow them to become the foundation of your life. A past issue is just one of the many things that happened to help you grow. You don't need to know why it happened. You don't need to analyze its cause and effect, from a karmic point of view. All sorts of things happen every day, and you don't understand why they happen. Yet you are comfortable handling them. You only insist on understanding the events that you can't comfortably handle. Understanding becomes a crutch, a source of rationalization. If the mind can't fit an event into its conceptual model, it insists on knowing why it happened. Better to accept reality first, then work with it in a constructive manner.

You are the Self. You are the conscious witness of all that passes before you. You dwell deep inside, and nothing in there is more powerful than you. You have free will; use it to accept what has already happened rather than letting past events mess up the rest of your life. Free yourself from these samskaras. Transmute your blocked energy flow into a powerful spiritual force.

CHAPTER 37

The Power of Intent

You are capable of letting go at a very deep level if you really want to. It is not a question of ability; it depends on intensity of intent. Inner work is different from outer work. In the outside world, there are things you may not be able to accomplish because of physical limitations. Try as you will, you cannot pick up a mountain or run at the speed of light. You have physical limitations. But inside you have no such limitations because there is no physical aspect to Self. You are pure consciousness, and your will has complete dominion over mind and emotions.

As we have seen, most of your thoughts and emotions are created by the blockages you have stored inside. These blockages are yours, and you can let them go anytime you want. Once again, the problem is that since they were stored with pain, they are going to release with pain. That is where the depth of commitment comes in. Do you want to be free to live a deep, beautiful life more than you want to avoid discomfort? Plenty of drug addicts have gone through the pain of withdrawal to get their lives back. It comes down to the old adage: where there's a will, there's a way. You can let your blockages go—if you really want to. What would you be willing to go through for the most fulfilling love relationship, a constant state of well-being, and the ability to feel the presence of God flowing through you at all times? How would you answer? Would you say, "I'm too busy and I don't like any discomfort"? Or would you meet the challenge and say, "Anything. I would be willing to go through anything to permanently live in such a state"? Fortunately, you have the ability; that is not the problem. But do you have the strength of intent to take the deep spiritual journey to liberation?

Will is like a muscle—you build it by exercising it. Practice saying, "I'm the boss in here. This is my house. I'm the only one living in here, and I have the right to make it a nice place to live." It's not about becoming a control freak in there—it's about learning to surrender. Surrender is not about suppression, and it's not about control. Surrender is about letting go of weakness and being committed enough to carry out your intent. Surrender is handling anything that needs to be released inside and letting it pass through. Remember, it was you who willfully resisted past events, which caused samskaras to be stored. Why not learn to willfully relax and release as the blockages cleanse so you can experience the beautiful inner energy flow as it is meant to be?

If you practice letting go of your blockages, not only will you get to live in an elevated inner state, you will also become a blessing on the Earth. Anyplace you go, anything you do, will carry a blessing for others. If you stay with this process every day, you will get there. Put time aside to remind yourself who you are and to recall your commitment to cleaning up inside. Morning and evening practices will help you do this. It doesn't have to be much time; just enough to relax and release, come back to center, and remember to use every moment of your life to let go of your blockages. If you do that, the rest will happen by itself. It is a natural process that will take place.

Always remember, it is spirit's job to liberate you from yourself. Shakti wants to be free, but you're in the way. When shakti starts to push the blockages up, you're going to have the tendency to push them back down because it's not comfortable to live in that fire. You stored past disturbances in there, and it doesn't feel good when they are stirred up. Imagine that somebody's talking to you, and you're feeling strong and confident about the conversation. Suddenly, they say something that hits your blockages, and you start to feel your strength drop out from under you. If you are sincere, you use the situation for your growth. It's not the time to argue with the person; it's the time to grow spiritually. Calm and centered, you inwardly ask, "What's happening inside of me? What blockage got hit that caused this shift in energy to take place?" Then, to use the situation for growth, you relax and allow the energy to push the blockage up. You don't have to do anything except not interfere with the process. Shakti will do her job of pushing up—you have to do your job of letting go.

To remember to do this in the moment, establish the practice of recalling your intention every morning: "The purpose of my day is letting go of my blockages and evolving spiritually." Then every evening, remember: "The purpose of my day was to let go of my blockages and evolve spiritually." Never complain about what happened—just inwardly release the events of the day so they don't leave samskaras. Don't let anything remain stuck in there. Once you get good at this, you will learn to do it throughout the day. Do your best with each interaction, then let it go. Always remember what's going on: you're in there, and something is happening that's causing the energy to shift inside. Your tendency is to push it away if you don't like it or grab onto it if you do. It's as if you have hands in there, and you use them to try to control the inner experience. Surrender means—don't do that. That's all it means. It means you're ready, willing, and able to sit in the seat of consciousness when the energy shifts and just let it go.

Your interaction with the energy is similar to when you decide to stop smoking or break any other habit. You're going to feel the tendency to resume the habit. It feels like a magnetic pull on you to go in that direction. The same thing happens when a blockage gets hit. It has attractive power that draws you into it. You need to see that. You need to notice that it keeps pulling on you, and sometimes it won't leave you alone. That's not bad, that's good. Just relax more. It's all about relaxing. If you're using your will to relax, you can't use your inner hands to push energy away or grab onto it.

Someday, you're going to remember this discussion. Something is going to wake up inside, and you'll know just what we've been talking about. You'll observe the energy pulling on you, and you will try to let go. For the first time you'll realize what is actually happening—you are struggling with yourself. You are both sides of the struggle. Part of you wants to let go but part still wants to give in to the pull of the energy. Once you sincerely want to let go of the old habitual energy flows, you will realize that you have all the power you need inside. You're the only one living in there. You just need to deeply relax and stop fighting with yourself. At that point something amazing is going to happen: All the energy that was pulling you down and out changes direction. It begins to lift you in and up. This is the transmutation of the energy, and it is real. As liberation becomes the meaning of your life, this inner process will step up significantly. Once you learn that your center of intent is stronger than any of the habitual energy flows caused by your samskaras, you will sit quietly within, in the seat of consciousness, and allow the process of purification to take place. Every day, every moment, you have the opportunity to explore the greatness of your being.

Letting go like this is not a struggle or an act of control. It is much subtler than that. Perhaps this analogy will help. Imagine you're in a game of tug-of-war. You are alone on one end of the rope, and an entire NFL football team is on the other end. You're in big trouble. The force pulling you in the team's direction is very strong. You've studied all the latest techniques for how to dig in your heels, how to best use your bodyweight, and anything else the experts could teach about standing your ground in a tug-of-war. You're doing all the techniques, but they're not working.

Suddenly, Yoda, the great sage from *Star Wars* shows up to help (he thinks everyone's name is Luke).

Yoda: Luke, you know not how to do this. Let go. Let go, Luke.

Luke: What do you mean, let go? If I let go, they will pull me through the mud, headfirst.

Yoda: Let go, you must.

Luke: I don't get it. How do I just let go when this great force is pulling on me?

Yoda: Relax hands, Luke. Relax your hands.

Luke: No, not hands—feet, legs, and body position. That's how to end this tug-of-war.

Yoda: Over it will be, Luke, if you relax your hands.

Turns out, it's true. If you relax your hands during a tug-of-war, the struggle will immediately be over. No more rope. No more pull. No matter how strong the pull is, if you relax your hands, you can go home and have lunch. That's all you really wanted to begin with. Who said you had to take the whole football team home with you? Just relax and let go, and the whole struggle will be over. That's exactly what it's like to surrender. You're in there, and the energy is pulling you into it. Please don't fight it. Just relax your inner hands and let go. If this sounds very Zen, good, because it is. You don't need to be strong; you need to be wise. The blocked energy can't take you anywhere if you simply relax and let go.

Over time, you will find there is a place inside you that is behind the commotion of the storm. You can simply relax and fall back into that place. This is the place from which you are noticing the inner commotion, and this place is still, quiet, and there are never any storms. That is the seat of Self. *You don't find your way back to Self—you simply cease to leave.* If you work on this, you will come to a beautiful state within that is always there for you. It is a place of refuge, and all you ever need to do is keep letting go. That is the life of surrender.

CHAPTER 38

Exploring the Higher States

Once you are no longer drowning inside, a whole other life becomes possible for you. We can now begin to discuss who you are, and what it can be like in there. As the blockages release, the energy is freed from having to go around them. You start to feel happier. You start to feel higher. You start to feel like you used to feel when you had a really good day or a particularly great experience. But this time, nothing special is happening. You're just feeling an uplifting energy going on inside of you that keeps getting higher and higher. You start feeling love simply because the sky is blue. It used to take a special moment in a relationship to blow you away like that. Everything that is happening comes in, and you feel it all at a richer, deeper level. This is because you are more open, more receptive. You don't have the needs and problems that you were trying to solve. Because you don't have all that commotion inside, and you're feeling more whole and complete, there's nothing you need from the outside. You start to look at needs in a completely different light.

You used to make satisfying needs your priority. Most of our modern needs are psychological, not physiological. Psychological needs are actually unnatural, as they indicate that something is missing or wrong. If you are feeling whole and complete inside yourself, there are no psychological needs. Psychological needs come from your blockages. When the energy is freed, what you feel is love, joy, and enthusiasm, which are just different words for uplifting energy. In the purest sense, this upward-flowing energy is quite different from emotions. An emotion emanates out of your heart and pulls you into its vibration. Enthusiasm is something that wells up inside. It is a system-wide, spontaneous, uplifting flow of energy. It is, in fact, freed shakti.

When your energies are liberated, you don't need energy from anybody else. You have so much energy inside you it's incomprehensible. Surely you have experienced from time to time that if something you really like happens, there can be a sudden burst of inner energy. How long does that take? A billionth of a second. Imagine you're feeling depressed and not doing well. Suddenly, something happens. Perhaps you receive a phone call that gets you talking and smiling—it makes your energy flow. The energy was always there, but you opened up because the phone call matched something you liked. A blockage temporarily got out of the way, and all this energy flowed up. Truth is, if that blockage had not been in the way, you would not have needed the phone call to open you. This is why you do the inner work of releasing blockages.

As the blockages release, the energy takes you to higher and higher states. You already know what the higher states are. The higher states are about love. They are about being really enthusiastic about your job and anything else you're doing. The higher energies are beautiful. They're much more beautiful than the expression of the lower energies. As you open up, life is no longer about seeking nonnegative states; it becomes about allowing ever-increasing, positive states. Growth used to be about not feeling anger or anxiety anymore. Now it's about feeling so much overwhelming love when you wake up that you have trouble getting out of bed. Then the feeling of enthusiasm to go to work gets so strong that it pulls you out of bed and propels you through your day. This is what it feels like when the energy is flowing.

Most people don't believe life can be like this. They feel they must find the perfect job in order to be enthused to go to work. How are you defining "the perfect job"? You define it as the one that opens you. In other words, the one that fits your blockages just right so your energy can flow. Problem is, if the same job ever hits your blockages the wrong way, you will close. You are still letting your samskaras run your life. It's not a matter of finding the right job; it's a matter of releasing the blockages so you can be enthused about the job you have.

No matter how high you get, you can always get much higher. Don't believe those who say you can't enjoy happiness unless you also know sadness. That is not true. That's what life is like if you are still blocked. Once you're unblocked, you will notice the energy is always beautiful. It is an ever-new rush of uplifting joy that raises your heart, your mind, and everything inside you. You'll be more aware than you used to be and have the enthusiasm of a child about everything you get to do.

You might wonder why you would be motivated to do anything if you're already that content. Why bother having a job, or even a relationship, if you're already filled with so much love and happiness? The answer is simple: love wants to express itself and enthusiasm wants to create. Once the energy is no longer blocked and is flowing freely, personal needs are no longer your motivation. Your actions are the expression of love and gratitude for life. Your whole life becomes an act of service.

Even your relationships become acts of service to other human beings. You don't need anything from a relationship, but love loves to express itself. If you have tremendous love going on inside you, people will be attracted to you. You don't have to worry about attracting somebody or keeping them interested in you. People are attracted to light. It's very natural. If there is someone special, you shower them with love day and night, expecting nothing in return. Love is a very unique gift—it is just as beautiful for both the giver and the receiver.

Life is so simple once you are okay inside. You don't do things because of the fruits they bear; each moment is whole and complete within itself. You reach the point where there is nothing more sacred than the spirit flowing inside you. There can be moments of disturbance, but you don't have to do anything about them. They come and they go, and they don't affect your energy flow, unless you let them. You will come to realize that this energy inside you knows what it's doing. It is not only beautiful, it is intelligent. If you let it, it will fix everything. The uprising energy will do all the inner work for you. Your only job is to not interfere—to surrender.

Let's go even deeper to explore what happens next. The energy flowing inside you is so beautiful that your consciousness is naturally attracted to it. What you are experiencing is everything you ever hoped to feel from the outside but could only taste for a moment. You fall completely in love with the spiritual energy flow. Once you're being fed by the inner flow, your outer life will be fine. Before you cleared the blockages, you needed the world to be a certain way for you to be okay. This created a struggle with life on a daily basis. When you let go enough to clear the inner energy flow, the struggling ceases. You realize through direct experience that everything you ever wanted is flowing inside you, and the battle will pretty much be over.

Attraction to the unconditional flow of inner energy is a wonderful love affair. In fact, the Bible says, "And thou shalt love the Lord thy God with all thine heart, and with all thy soul, and with all thy might" (Deut. 6:5). Now, you do. That is the ultimate commandment in the Old Testament, and Jesus repeated it many times. You no longer have to worry about how to "love God" because what's flowing inside of you is spirit, and you naturally love it with all your heart. You like being high, and spirit is the ultimate high. It's higher than any drug could ever take you. It's higher than any relationship you could ever have. The love and joy it brings will never stop unless you stop it. That river will flow every moment of your life unless you dam it up. But now you know better. Once the energy starts spontaneously flowing, you won't touch it. You just respect it, honor it, and appreciate it. You inwardly say, "Thank you," and keep letting go. That becomes your only prayer—*thank you, thank you so much.*

Now that this energy is flowing inside you, it will clean up the rest of your blockages. This will not happen immediately; you must be willing to let them go naturally. The shakti will push the samskaras out if you let her. Your entire life becomes spiritual—about spirit. You rest into the beautiful flow of the energy, and it gives you the strength to let go of what needs to be cleansed. In time, you learn to enjoy every moment of this journey. It is freeing you, taking you to God.

When you are settling into the upward flow of energy, that is a state of true contentment. Contentment doesn't mean you're lazy. It means you are not being disturbed inside. What is going on inside you is so beautiful that, for the first time in your life, you feel completely at peace. You're not looking for anything. If you look out into the world, you see what's there—not what you want or don't want to be there. The experience of the outside doesn't stimulate any preferences inside of you. It just comes in, passes through, and leaves you as it found you—in a state of ecstatic well-being.

CHAPTER 39

In the World but Not of It

Once you have reached a deep level of inner clarity, you will notice that just because you are content with reality doesn't mean you don't interact with it. The world continues to appear before you, but there's nothing personal about it anymore. It is just the part of creation passing before you at that moment. Reality doesn't bother you because you don't need anything from it. It simply exists and you simply exist—in perfect harmony. Every moment unfolding in front of you is there for you to serve. It can be as simple as appreciating it, or you may be able to raise the energy of the moment passing before you. A smile, a kind word, a helping hand—these are all ways of raising the energy as it passes by. Doing your job to the best of your ability, taking care of your family, serving your community—these simple acts are just as much service to the universe as anything else.

Imagine you're taking a walk and there's a piece of paper on the side of the road. You feel the disharmony, and you pick it up. It's not a "have to" or a "supposed to"; you're simply an artist making the world more beautiful. Your mind doesn't say, "I'll pick this one up, but I'm not going to pick up every single piece of litter." Nor does your mind say, "What idiot threw this piece of paper down here? This is the kind of person who ruins the world." No. You are simply a spontaneous being who is in harmony with life. You expect nothing back from your actions because they were not done for approval or recognition. You can't help but share the beautiful energy going on inside of you with the moment in front of you. *The highest life you can live is when every single moment that passes before you is better off because it did.* Serve the present moment with all your heart and soul. Imagine what the world would be like if everyone did that.

Start by raising what appears before you. If you can't even serve what is put in front of you, how are you going to change the world? If you are getting so upset about conditions in the world that you're edgy with everyone around you, you're not helping anyone. If you can't create harmony in your own household, what right do you have to complain that countries are shooting missiles at each other? You have to live a life that, if everyone lived it, there would be peace. If you can't do that, you are part of the problem, not the solution. It's all about letting go of yourself. The world is going to come in, and it's going to hit what's left of your samskaras. What you feel going on inside when that happens is reactive energy. Don't ever act based on that. You will just be polluting the environment with your inner blockages. No good can come from that.

A spiritual life is not about adhering to a given set of rules—it's about never acting based on your personal energy. You won't be able to do that to start with, so work on it. When the energy gets disturbed, just let it go. Your initial reaction will generally be your personal stuff coming up. If you let it go, you'll be able to interact with the moment in front of you in a more constructive manner. Simply ask yourself, "Is there something I can be doing to serve the moment in front of me? Not for me; I already let go of me. Now that I'm clear and nonreactive, is there something I can do to raise the moment as it passes by?"

Once you learn to let go of the reactionary noise of personal thoughts and emotions, things will become clear. You will know how to work with the situation in front of you. If you're conscious, present, and paying attention, you will know what to do. The moment in front of you is talking to you. It doesn't have to be in words. The piece of paper on the ground, the person who needs some help, whatever it is, your response becomes obvious. The deepest truth is that it doesn't even matter what you do. What matters is where you're coming from. What matters is your motive. If your motive is to let go of yourself and serve the moment in front of you, you are worthy of great respect. How would you like to meet somebody whose entire motive and purpose in life is to first let go of their personal blockages and then do their best to serve what's in front of them? They can't do wrong because their motive is pure. If the motive itself is pure and impersonal, in the end, it will spread light.

Be sure your motive is pure, then don't look back. If somebody criticizes your actions, just apologize and let go. Always be willing to learn. If you come from the highest place you can, there's no guilt, no shame. The fruits of the best you can do are a very holy thing. If something terrible comes back from the best you can do, own it. It's yours. Let it teach you. Let it make you better, so you'll do better next time. Please, don't feel bad about it. Don't judge anything. It's only when you didn't do your best— you got personally disturbed and gave in to it—that's when you build karma and things become really complicated.

Practice letting go, and eventually you will find yourself in a seat of awareness that can't be disturbed by anything you are experiencing. There will always be a beautiful energy feeding you and raising you. At that point, there are no more techniques; there are no more teachings. It all happens naturally from then on. Intuitively, it dawns on you that this beautiful energy flow must be coming from somewhere. Yogananda wrote in *Whispers from Eternity* (1949, 156), "O, what has become of me? Intoxication on intoxication! Endless, indescribable throngs of divine intoxications ceaselessly come to me!" Where is this energy coming from? You feel it as a flow, just as if rushes of water were flowing upward within you. This is not theoretical, it's real. There is a constant experience of shakti, of spirit flowing up inside you. It must be coming from somewhere. It has to have a source. You are now ready for the next stage of your journey home—you begin to seek the source.

You will very quickly realize the mind cannot help you on this journey. Any focus on thoughts draws consciousness away from Self and diminishes the energy flow. This is not an analytical or philosophical journey. Only one thing can seek the source of the energy flow: that which is experiencing it—your consciousness. To seek the source of a freshwater spring, you swim toward the flow. You feel the current and go into it. It is the same when you are seeking the source of the shakti flow.

Your consciousness feels the flow and melts into it. This becomes your entire spiritual practice. This is surrender, real surrender.

Heretofore, you've practiced surrender by letting go of your lower self. Now that you've learned to feel this higher energy flow inside, you surrender to it. Until this final surrender, there is still a subject-object experience: consciousness (subject) is experiencing the shakti flow (object). If you want to truly know the flow, you must fall into it, become one with it.

To get closer to becoming one with flow, you must surrender your entire sense of separation. It's not enough to experience the energy, you must release yourself into it. As you let go, the flow will pull you in. That's where the great masters went. In Sanskrit, the word *yoga* means "union." Meher Baba said that when he first went into the highest state of enlightenment, it was like a drop of water fell into the ocean. Try to find that drop. You can't—it merged with the ocean. Christ said, "I and my Father are one" (John 10:30). These teachings are the same. When you cease to separate your sense of self from this flow of the energy, it starts to pull you into it, and you become one with it. Yogananda called it a river of joy flowing inside you. Your path is to find it, go there, get in, and drown. Now we're discussing the highest state, and everyone is capable of achieving this state.

Remember how we got here. We got here by letting go of the blockages to this flow. The higher states are totally natural, but you shouldn't be seeking them. Don't be blocked and then try to experience what it's like to not be blocked. Get unblocked and the deeper meditations will come completely naturally. You'll be minding your own business watching TV, and you'll fall into states that you couldn't reach after hours of meditation. You will become a being of shakti, and she will take you into ecstasy over and over again.

There is nothing more beautiful than the shakti flow. She is so fulfilling that you would never block her again. If something happens and you feel you want to defend yourself, don't touch it. First let go of the part of you that wants to close down, then deal with the outside. Use everything to let go of what stands between you and the God-realized state.

Start with the low-hanging fruit throughout the day and then progress to letting go of your past. That's a perfect way to begin meaningful transformation. Once you learn how to let go of self-generated disturbances, inevitably something bigger will happen. Because of the work you have done on yourself, it will be totally natural for you to let go during more challenging times. Don't wait until a terrible bomb goes off in your life to wonder what to do differently. You need to do the work of releasing yourself in your everyday life. You will then be able to handle anything life brings your way.

Like most things in life, these deeper spiritual states take time. Just do the inner work, and the energy will start flowing. Once the floodgates open within you, you'll have all the help you need for the ascent. You are not walking this path alone—all who walked before you are lifting you. Just keep letting go. No matter what happens, keep letting go. These states are not going to happen all at once and then stay there. You'll get rushes from time to time because something opens up. It's okay if it closes back down; don't worry. You still have work to do. Be diligent, but give it time. Eventually, the upward flow will never leave you. You will become a knower of your soul, a knower of spirit. When you can relax and release into the deeper states, you will finally awaken to full self-realization. That's what true enlightenment is. Enlightenment is not a spiritual experience—it is a permanent spiritual state.

No matter how deep you have gone, please do not say you're enlightened. Let that word be reserved for the great masters. Just be content. Don't build a spiritual ego. Spirituality is not about hanging out a shingle that says, "I'm a spiritual person." It is about letting go of that too. It is about perpetually letting go of yourself completely. If you never stop doing this, the energy will take over. Where you used to see your personal self expressing, you will now see nothing but the flow of shakti. Surrender to the flow. Give your life to it. Merge into it, and it will take you the rest of the way. That is the final surrender.

It has been such an honor to share these teachings with you. Please, don't let this be just another book you read and then go back to your normal way of life. Do this work. This work is not about renunciation of life—it's about truly experiencing life at the deepest level. If you let go of yourself on a daily basis, under all circumstances, you will find what is greater than yourself. That's just the way it works: Where you're not, God is. Where God is, you're not.

Now do you understand why Christ said the Kingdom is within you? It is the very essence of your being. Your heights are incomprehensible, and you are perfectly capable of doing this work. Your inner states will just keep getting higher and higher as you keep letting go. The fact that you are even interested in these teachings means you've changed the world. You who do the work of liberating yourself are to be deeply respected.

With great love and respect,

Michael A. Singer

Acknowledgments

Life is a great teacher. If you are open, every single situation has something to teach you about yourself and the moment unfolding in front of you. I begin by acknowledging how much this flow of life has taught me and has led to the writing of *Living Untethered*. I also acknowledge all those wise beings who have walked this path before me and managed to guide me on my exploration within.

It is with deep humility and appreciation that I recognize the tremendous work that my friend and product manager, Karen Entner, did on this book. Her tireless and selfless service has instilled this work with a sense of commitment and perfection rarely found in this world.

I would also like to take this opportunity to thank my publishers, New Harbinger Publications and Sounds True, for their heartfelt work in bringing *Living Untethered* to fruition. They worked together seamlessly to meld their great talents into one unified force behind the development, marketing, and distribution of this very special book.

There were many early readers, all of whom deserve thanks. I would like to single out James O'Dea, Bob Merrill, and Stephanie Davis, who contributed detailed suggestions during the early writing of the book.

Lastly, I would like to acknowledge you, the reader, for being interested in deepening your relationship with yourself and the world around you. Your willingness to take a second look at what is really going on, outside and in, has the power to change the world.

About the Author

 **MICHAEL A. SINGER** is author of the #1 *New York Times* bestseller, *The Untethered Soul*, and the *New York Times* bestseller, *The Surrender Experiment*, both of which have been published worldwide. He had a deep inner awakening in 1971 while working on his doctorate in economics, and went into seclusion to focus on yoga and meditation. In 1975, he founded Temple of the Universe, a now long-established yoga and meditation center where people of any religion or set of beliefs can come together to experience inner peace. Along with his nearly five decades of spiritual teaching, Singer has made major contributions in the areas of business, education, health care, and environmental protection.

» Visit untetheredsoul.com for more information about Michael A. Singer and his books, including *The Surrender Experiment*

» Explore articles and interviews with Michael A. Singer at: untetheredsoul.com/news

» Hear Michael A. Singer read from *The Untethered Soul* at: newharbinger.com/tus

» Watch an in-depth INTERVIEW with Michael A. Singer at: bit.ly/tusinterview

» Find AUDIO TALKS by Michael A. Singer at: store.untetheredsoul.com

Read the #1 *New York Times* bestseller by Michael A. Singer

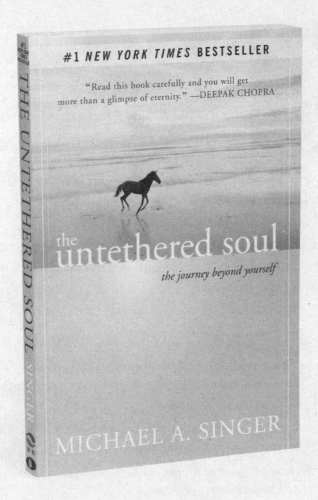

Who are you really? What would it be like to free yourself from limitations and soar beyond your boundaries? What can you do each day to discover inner peace and serenity? *The Untethered Soul* has helped millions of readers find the answers to these profound questions.

$18.95 / ISBN 9781572245372

More ways to experience
The Untethered Soul

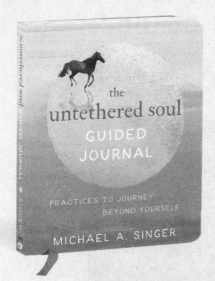

A Guided Journal
A color-illustrated journal to help you discover inner peace, freedom, and joy.

$19.95 / ISBN 9781684036561

A Special Gift Edition
A beautiful hardcover with ribbon bookmark—makes a perfect gift anytime of year!

$24.95 / ISBN 9781626250765

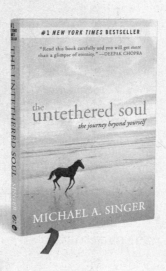

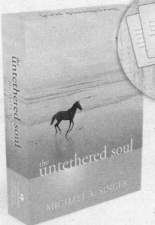

A 52-Card Deck
These extraordinary cards feature profound and uplifting quotes to inspire you!

$17.95 / ISBN 9781684034314

A POWERFUL,
FREE MINI-COURSE
WITH
MICHAEL A. SINGER

Join the bestselling author of *The Untethered Soul* and *The Surrender Experiment* for a **FREE** three-part video series to transform the way you relate to your own mind.

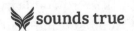

https://qrco.de/soundstrue